Contents

OXFORD
BLACKWELL SCIENTIFIC PUBLICATIONS
LONDON EDINBURGH BOSTON
MELBOURNE PARIS BERLIN VIENNA

This book is dedicated to my three children Andy, Rosalind, and Hal who are themselves very creative and special people.

© Sue Jennings 1993

Blackwell Scientific Publications
Editorial Offices:
Osney Mead, Oxford OX2 0EL
25 John Street, London WC1N 2BL
23 Ainslie Place, Edinburgh EH3 6AJ
238 Main Street, Cambridge,
   Massachusetts 02142, USA
54 University Street, Carlton,
   Victoria 3053, Australia

Other Editorial Offices:
Librairie Arnette SA
2, rue Casimir-Delavigne
75006 Paris
France

Blackwell Wissenschafts-Verlag GmbH
Meinekestrasse 4
D-1000 Berlin 15
Germany

Blackwell MZV
Feldgasse 13
A-1238 Wien
Austria

First published 1993

Set by Best-set Typesetter Ltd,
Hong Kong
Printed and bound in Great Britain

DISTRIBUTORS
Marston Book Services Ltd
PO Box 87
Oxford OX2 0DT
(*Orders*: Tel: 0865 791155
          Fax: 0865 791927
          Telex: 837515)

USA
Blackwell Scientific Publications, Inc.
238 Main Street
Cambridge, MA 02142
(*Orders*: Tel: 800 759-6102
                617 876-7000)

Canada
Times Mirror Professional Publishing, Ltd
130 Flaska Drive
Markham, Ontario L6G 1B8
(*Orders*: Tel: 800 268-4178
                416 470-6739)

Australia
Blackwell Scientific Publications Pty Ltd
54 University Street
Carlton, Victoria 3053
(*Orders*: Tel: 03 347-5552)

British Library
Cataloguing in Publication Data
A Catalogue record for this book is
available from the British Library

ISBN 0-632-02442-9

Library of Congress
Cataloging in Publication Data
available

Foreword

As every student of the science of development knows, play is a serious business. *Playtherapy with Children* describes and explains play with children as an understandable and coherent area of theoretical knowledge, as a professional activity, and as a personal experience for the practitioner, the reader, and for Dr Jennings herself.

For among the powerful impressions this book conveys, two stand out. First, there is the presence of the author, neither dimmed nor distorted by the myriad academic and technical processes which stand between writer and reader. In many ways the book comes across like a personal tutorial with Sue Jennings. Or, rather, a series of tutorials, because for all its playfulness, and its return again and again to the experiences and practicalities of what play-therapist and child actually do together, the book covers a great deal of ground. Again and again, the setting is the same: Adult and Child; yet at the same time the writer and the reader of this book travel a long way together.

The other impression is, for me, very close to Sue Jennings' particular contribution to creative therapy. Play in all its forms, for example in the best of science and the arts, can connect the everyday with the sublime in a way that matters, and takes people to their highest achievements. Yet it is possible for therapists who use the arts to be drawn too much in another direction, into psychological structures and ideology which, in the end, are reductionist rather than liberating and creative.

There is real pain and danger in work with emotionally troubled

or injured people of any age, and comfort and security in the
words, rules and rituals of the therapeutic heroes, and every
therapist is drawn, more or less, towards the built-in props and
supports of clinical work. Sue Jennings is one of the relatively few,
in my experience, who successfully perform the acrobatic task
of achieving a balance between both, the necessary playfulness,
openness, humanity and risks of play and the arts, and the equally
necessary caution, carefulness and limitations of therapy.

This book conveys Sue Jennings' skill and experience in strad-
dling these two worlds in a way that is both creative and therapeutic, and in a style which (like the high-wire act) may look more
simple and straightforward than it is – by which I mean it is a
readable and enjoyable book, with depth. It is a stimulating and
instructive addition to the literature of play and creative therapies.

Derek Steinberg
Consultant in Child and Adolescent Psychiatry
The Maudsley and Bethlem Royal Hospitals

Preface

Most of my writing and practice has been about dramatherapy and drama and I have always taken the significance of play as implicit in the development of drama. The play of children is the basis both of drama and of the capacity for human beings to create and re-create. What we witness as theatre as adults – whether as entertainment, culture or political statement – has emerged from our capacity to exercise our dramatic imagination, to suspend our disbelief, and to react 'as if' a fiction is true. The dramatic imagination, whether acted upon or whether confined to what goes on in our heads, is an essential part of being a human being – of being a person.

Although I know that the healthy development of human beings and their culture is seriously influenced by dramatic play and drama, I realize that increased attention needs to be paid to the fundamentals of play and playtherapy in their own right as well as their role as a precursor to drama and dramatherapy. There are plenty of theories on child development as manifested in play, and every theorist has something to contribute to our understanding of the importance of playtherapy and its application. I hope that this book, by its practical nature, can offer a playtherapy method that can be applied with children in distress of many different kinds.

There is perhaps a particular urgency for a book of this nature now that we are so much more aware of the extent of childhood trauma in our society. Through the various agencies it is now possible as never before for children to communicate their distress rather than staying quiet and carrying the burden into their adult lives – often with permanent psychological damage. The earlier damaging experiences can be communicated, the better for the healthy survival of the child. However, it is also important to emphasize the preventative values of play. As children are able to play, they are also able to help themselves – to develop their own repair system as a self-regulator of experience. The child who is able to play will have more resources to draw on, both in childhood and in adult life.

I have tried in this book to draw on the importance of both preventative play and curative play. Some curative play can happen spontaneously, of course, but it is at times necessary for the play-therapist to intervene. All human beings have the capacity to play and the capacity to dramatize. The extent to which these capacities are developed and sustained is influenced by culture, family, and education; there can also be variation within a single culture. As indicated in UK culture, play and drama come fairly low down in the prioritizing of resources: pre-school provision for children is still minimal. In addition, it is caught up in the debate about whether mothers should work rather than being part of a wider world of play being good for children. Drama, likewise, is not seen as an essential part of the school curriculum – even as a means of learning other subjects such as history or languages let alone in its own right.

The aim of this book is to demonstrate the fundamental importance of play, not just as children but continuously throughout our lives. Human play covers a very wide area of human activity; it can mature into the arts and sports but *it also needs to carry on in its own right*. The capacity to be playful – whether with ideas, with a relationship, with a crisis – enables us to manage life more appropriately and more creatively.

People often comment that play is not important because it is not *real* – something which is also said about drama! The reverse is in fact true. Because play and drama are not 'real', they are therefore *crucial* to human survival. It is necessary for all of us to have the capacity to imagine how life is or could be, to be able to call into mind what is not there and does not exist. How many great ideas and experiments have started from the dramatic ingredients of sheer human survival. They can also be part of re-parenting, repair and reparation for those who have been damaged – as individuals, families or groups.

The foreword and afterword of this book have been undertaken by two people for whom I have great respect as people and as professionals. Derek Steinberg, a consultant in adolescent psychiatry, is a clinician with whom I have worked over some years in both the UK and Greece. His work with children, adolescents and families has always made me hopeful about the basic sensibility of any therapeutic intervention, and inspired my own work in relation to the synthesis between the creative and the clinical. Peter Slade has been a stimulus for over twenty years in his work in Child Drama and especially through his concept of projective play and personal play. Many of us now working as dramatherapists would not be doing so if it were not for Peter's indefatigable pioneering work.

Finally, there is an appendix with useful addresses as well as an extended bibliography.

It is my hope that this book will assist the creative journey of both playtherapists and their children so that both child and adult may find both security and magic in their world again.

Sue Jennings
Stratford-upon-Avon

Acknowledgements

This is the first time that I have written a proportion of my own experience into my work and there are several people already mentioned in the text to whom I owe a great deal in terms of my development and growth – Peter Slade, the late Veronica Sherborne, Dorothy Heathcote, Gavin Bolton and Brian Way, and all those in the early drama-in-education field. The writings of Alice Miller are also very important to me.

I must thank all those in The Institute of Dramatherapy, whether trainee, staff, advisor or trustee, and also the people who are starting the new Association of Play Therapists. Trainees and clients are always there to stimulate new pathways and provide ideas – I owe them so much in terms of the content of this book.

I wish to extend my personal thanks to the following people who provide me with continuing professional and personal support: Ann Cattanach, Murray Cox, Hugh and Jean Dickinson, Audrey Hillyar, Mooli Lahad, Robert Silman and Gordon Wiseman.

Pictures re-drawn by Audrey Hillyar. The photograph on p. 112 by George Solomonides. The developmental checklist in Appendix 1 is adapted from Richard Courtney's 'Drama Assessment; Appendix' (1981) in *Drama in Therapy. Volume 1 – Children* (Ed. by G. Schattner and R. Courtney). New York: Drama Book Specialists. Richard Courtney is Professor of Arts and Education, Ontario Institute for Studies and Education, Toronto, Canada.

Introduction

Play is a very personal activity. People play from their earliest months of life and continue to do so in some form or other until they go to the big playground in the sky.

This book on playtherapy is another step on my own personal and professional life journey that I hope will grow by being shared with you the reader. The experience of play and especially dramatic play, has steered me through many a troubled time both as a child and then an adult. I was brought up in a very strict yet eccentric medical family where reality was always the reality of logic. The logic of the imagination was something I discovered when life got too tough for a 4 year old and I had wonderful escapes into my own play and stories.

Of course for a 'war child', new mythologies grew up of contemporary heroes and villains and stories were enacted in our front garden with the local children until they were scared away by the doctor's needle. My experience is probably very typical of my generation yet perhaps it was exacerbated by my parents' reluctance to send their children to school. The school of life – which meant the school of my parents' life – was the lens through which we were to view the world. However, when you miss out on school games, you invent your own games to play. When there is not a club to join, you create a society that you can then become a member of. It was through all these experiences that I realized that play was like a survival kit for my own emotional health.

And of course when I had my own children, although I do not rate myself very highly as a parent, nevertheless we were able to play a lot and I had my creative needs met too. The big adventure for us as a family was when we all went to live in the Malaysian rain forest (a story that is being told at length elsewhere). I was doing my doctoral research on healing theatre and midwifery, and my three children came with me. We were adopted into the tribe and lived their way of life and learned about the importance of play and drama in people's lives.

The Temiar tribe allowed children to be children, and play lasted until puberty when people would usually marry. So either you were a child, or you were fertile and producing children, otherwise you were older and therefore wise.

They regularly had dramatic seances for both healing and prevention. There was music, singing, dancing and dramatisation in these rituals and they were the focus of the social and psychological life of the community. It was also very important that individuals could find their voice with the collective through their artistic endeavours.

Most of my adult life has been spent in attempting to develop the therapy inherent in play and drama. My book *Remedial Drama*, published some 20 years ago, was a first step in communicating some of my basic beliefs, which in the main had been learned from my own experience, to other people. It is a measure of its success that the book stayed around for many years. However when I look at it now, I see how much the playful world has moved on.

During my adult journey my work has been influenced by several special people who I must mention. Firstly the actor Harry Andrews who I met in my teens and who strengthened my resolve to keep trying! The early work of Peter Slade and Veronica Sherborne – both of whom I mention later in this book were enormous inspiration and influenced my formative time. Then there have been many people with whom I have both loved and fought – and curiously in the fighting I have had to sharpen my own thoughts towards clarity and understanding.

However at the end of it all, my playful life is similar to everyone else's playful life and mine is currently taking me back to play on the professional stage. By the time this book is published I shall have performed in at least two plays and there is a feeling that it is beginning to synthesize. My internal and external plays have a commonality and I perform them both for myself as well as other people.

Sue Jennings
Stratford-upon-Avon

Chapter 1

Human Developmental Stages (or Scenes)

INTRODUCTION TO SOME THEORIES OF HUMAN DEVELOPMENT

Each new decade brings new theories in relation to human development both as individuals and in groups. Some new theories incorporate previous theories, others purport to be a new theory. Some in fact turn out to be a new language for a previous theory. However, what is optimistic about the present is that there is a developing concept of a 'multi-model' approach (Lahad, 1992) which says that theories need not be mutually exclusive, and that new circumstances and phenomena will require new understanding or adaptation of old theory.

Every developmental theory will be based either on the orientation of the theorist (Freud, Jung or Klein, for example), or else on observed phenomena such as physical or cognitive skill, play and dramatic play (Piaget, Pulaski and Courtney, for example). Whereas the *orientation theorists* require that we accept the given basis for the theory, the *observational theorists* provide us with observations that relate tasks to age stages that we can readily apply to our work. To put this another way, orientation theorists not only observe phenomena but also attach explanations of their *meaning*; there is therefore usually an interpretative assumption concerning intra-psychic theory. By contrast, observational theorists do not emphasize the inner world of the child, but base their observations on external, observable progressions of achievement. These two broad categories that I have outlined above are not mutually exclusive but give a focus which can be useful in understanding the plethora of theories which exist, all based on developmental stages.

The purpose of this chapter is not to try to defend a particular orientation and theorist but to briefly summarize the innovative contributions to this debate. Neither do I intend to emphasize one set of observed skills more than another, but rather to give a description of the several task-based approaches to our greater understanding of the purpose and function of play and therefore playtherapy.

It is not within the remit of this chapter, or even this book as a whole, to enter into a philosophical debate on the nature of human beings and the world. However, it is important to point out that a fundamental way humans have of organizing our thinking is through developmental structure. One thing leads to another, as we say, and the 'one thing' can never be a totality of the person at any given moment in their growth, nor can any one theory successfully include all phenomena of a person's growth and development.

We can now consider, briefly, several theories of general human development and of play development which should assist us in grasping the importance of play for all human beings. These are considered (1) from the clinician's viewpoint; (2) in terms of developmental and dramatic play, (3) different play therapy approaches; and (4) in a discussion of the playtherapy method.

1. THE CLINICIAN'S VIEWPOINT OF CHILD DEVELOPMENT

Psychoanalysis and object relations orientation

Freud's classical theory of the libido emphasizes the psycho-sexual development of human beings, especially their individual development and gratification of needs. Like Erikson (whose work is discussed below), Freud suggests that there are eight phases in the life of a person:

(1)	Oral–sensory	0–1 years
(2)	Muscular–anal	1–3 years
(3)	Locomotor–genital (phallic–Oedipal)	3–5 years
(4)	Latency	6–puberty
(5)	Puberty and adolescence	

(6)   Young adulthood–genitality
(7)   Adulthood
(8)   Maturity

Freud describes mental functioning as taking place on two levels – the primary processes and the secondary processes – which he states are antagonistic to each other. The primary mental processes are characteristic of unconscious thought and include dreaming, symbolization and displacement, all of which largely determine human behaviour. This has further been characterized as follows:

'. . . a storehouse of unexpressed feelings and dark instinctual longings for sex, love, and power'.

(Landy, 1986: p. 18)

'Primary process thinking tends to be "iconic" (i.e. visual rather than verbal) and to disregard the laws of syntax, time and place'.

(Rycroft, 1985: p. 12)

The primary processes come from libidal sexual drives which are uncontrolled and unboundaried and are connected to Freud's theory of the pleasure principle.

The secondary processes are logical and rational and seek to keep in check the unbridled expressions of the unconscious. They are connected to the reality principle, that is the demands of the real and outside world.

The relationship between these primary and secondary processes and the inner and outer life are mediated, according to Freud, by a three-part 'psychic apparatus' – the id, ego and superego. Part of a child's development is the separation out of a healthy life-regulating ego from the pleasure seeking, instinctual id. This, Freud suggests, cannot come about until a child has moved through the early stages of oral/anal/phallic pleasure gratification.

Melanie Klein, whose major work was with children, was heavily influenced by Freud's thinking but nevertheless rejected some of his theory. In particular she discounted the idea of libidal stages of development and replaced them with her own theory of a succession of introjections and projections – i.e. feelings and wishes that are either internalized from the outside world or externalized from the internal world. Klein states that there are two crucial *positions* for the small infant that have to be successfully navigated; these are:

(1)   The paranoid–schizoid position
(2)   The depressive position

Unlike Freud, Klein believes that the baby already has sufficient ego at birth to build object relationships, in fantasy and reality, based on instinctual drives to satisfy needs. She believes that the paranoid–schizoid position is characterized by the infant splitting its experience of the 'good and bad breast'. The infant introjects the good breast and projects the bad breast.

> 'Her theory stresses the innate ambivalence between love and hate which, she maintains, derives from this basic opposition. She sees the destructive drives, sadism and aggression of the infant as being a defensive turning away from the self of this inherent, self-destructive death instinct. She focuses on how the infant supposedly copes with its overbearing instinctual drives in relation to the mother and her breast. But, for Klein, the infant emerges as truly monstrous, possessed by "phantasies" of sadistic destruction directed towards the mother's body.'
> (Rycroft, *ibid*: p. 15)

Kleinian theory believes that persecutory anxieties are suffered by the infant in relation to the mother and her breast at a few months of age. She interprets sucking and biting as symptomatic of the ambivalence between love and hate, that is, the life and death instincts of the child.

Projective identification is typical of this position, in which parts of the self and inner world are split off and projected into the outer world; identification then takes place with the projected parts. The infant is therefore struggling with the experience of both self and mother as loving and destructive objects.

The second phase, the depressive position, occurs after four months of age and for the remainder of the first year and this is when the infant's relationship to the outside world becomes more differentiated. Both the integration of the ego and the synthesis of good and bad produce depressive anxiety in the infant. The anxiety produces fear that the infant's destructive feelings can destroy the loved object, the mother/breast. Similarly, there is the emergence of guilt from the destructive feelings towards the good object.

Psychoanalytic thinking has moved from the purely instinctual theory to a more developed 'object relations' theory in which the relationship between objects has been given more prominence through the work of people such as Ferenczi, Balint, Winnicott and Guntrip.

Winnicott's theories, which will also be referred to later in the discussions on playtherapy, are embedded in a classical Freudian framework and they draw attention to the series of relationships that the child forms, as, for example:

(1) Mother's love expressed physically
(2) Mother's holding of a child in unintegrated state
(3) Mother and child in two-person relationship
(4) Mother, father and child in triangular relationship

According to Winnicott, in adequate surroundings, mothers go through a phase of 'primary maternal preoccupation' (Winnicott, 1975), which is similar to falling in love, her primary occupation being to satisfy the child's needs. As the mother's other interests return, this assists the child to develop a balance between satisfaction and frustration so that the child moves from being held by the mother in an unintegrated state, to a two-person relationship of mother and child, and then to the triangular relationship of the family. The child is then able to deal with more maturing relationships with siblings and other people outside the family.

Winnicott's unique contribution to the object–relations theory is the identification of what he terms 'transitional phenomena'. He believes that the child is assisted in its separation from the mother through phenomena that come to represent the mother, her presence, love and care, such as the 'security blanket' and, later, soft toys. Winnicott has observed that transitional phenomena act as a defence against anxiety between the ages of four and twelve months, where soft material is sucked, caressed, often accompanied by 'mum-mum' sounds. We shall look further at transitional phenomena and their relationship with early play activity later in this chapter.

Although Klein introduced the technique of play through which interpretations could be made about a child's unconscious world, it was Winnicott who recognized the importance of the playful and creative *relationship* between mother and child, and between therapist and client. Both however fit within the object-relations theoretical framework in relation to child development.

Jung and child psychotherapy

It is only comparatively recently that Jungian analytic psychologists have addressed the issue of therapy with children. Training now exists for Jungian child analysts as well as adult analysts. This has been made possible largely through the innovatory work of Michael Fordham who developed Jung's ideas of the self and individuation and also the idea of archetypes in relation to the developing child, something that had previously been considered only to apply to adults. Fordham postulates the presence of a child's *primary self* which goes through a process of deintegration and reintegration (Fordham, 1986). Until Fordham's work, the child had not been perceived of as a whole individual, but as being part of the mother.

Based on the principle that an infant grows from unconscious to conscious, Fordham claims that the process of deintegration is an archetypal one,

'Obviously these characteristics would not be those of myths but would be much more primitive; they would be in the nature of good and bad objects and there would be fusion of archetypal and real objects which the infant ego was not sufficiently developed to differentiate.'

(Fordham, 1986: p. 25)

Dora M. Kalff, a Jungian analyst, has written about her psycho-therapeutic approach to the psyche through 'sandplay' (Kalff, 1980), and she says that her sandplay observations have borne out the individuation processes described by Jung. She describes the stage of 'mother–child unity' where the child's experiences are of total safety and security. After one year, the Self of the child separates from the mother and a relationship of trust develops between mother and infant. The third phase, which occurs at the end of the second year is, according to Kalff, the stablization of the unconscious of the child – expressed through play, drawing and painting in the ancient language of symbols – the language of *wholeness*, i.e. circles or squares or human figures of 'godly content'. Kalff goes on to say:

'We accept the validity of these symbols of the wholeness of the human psyche because they have occurred everywhere without exception from the earliest times of man.'

(Kalff, 1980: p. 24)

Kalff goes on to discuss the emergence of the healthy ego and says that it can only develop on a basis of total security, i.e. when the manifestation of the Self occurs at 2–3 years. (According to Jung [1967], the Self consists of the 'sum of its conscious and unconscious, given facts [data], and that the Self directs the psychic developmental process from the time of birth.)

According to Kalff (*op cit*), when a weak ego is observed, the 'manifestation of the Self as a symbol' has not taken place at the usual developmental stage of 2–3 years. However, it can be 'recovered' in therapy, and through sandplay in particular. Kalff describes the three stages of ego development as postulated by Neumann (1973) and describes how they are depicted in sandplay therapy. These three stages are:

(1) The animal, vegetative stage
(2) The fighting stage
(3) The adaptation to the collective

> '. . . in the first phase, the ego expresses itself chiefly in pictures in which animals and vegetation predominate. The next stage brings battles, which appear again and again, especially in puberty. By now, the child is so strengthened that he can take upon himself the battle with external influences and he can come to grips with them. Finally he is admitted to the environment as a person and becomes a member of the collective.'
>
> (*op cit*: p. 33)

Jungian child therapists are distinguished by their mythic and spiritual frame of reference in relation to symbol and image and their emphasis on the essential wholeness of human beings. Nevertheless, as Fordham (1988) points out, care must be taken with the fusion hypothesis of the mythic 'ideal stage' to which can be attributed a state of total bliss. Fordham considers that Neumann (1973) was inspired by this idea and assumes that there is a period during the infant's first year where fusion takes place – known as the 'primal relationship' – where the mother actually *is* the infant's self. Fordham goes on to say:

> 'I consider his writing attractive, poetic and sometimes illuminating, but obscured by the application of a system derived from studies in mythology to such an extent that there is not reference to a real child from start to finish of his book; so the whole construction lacks reality.'
>
> (*op cit*: p. 27)

Perhaps this is the right moment to move on to other developmental theorists and their observations of play. However, while there is observation and analysis of the various component parts of human beings, it is reassuring to remember Kalff's emphasis:

'. . . the manifestation of the Self, this inner order, this pattern for wholeness, is the most important moment in the development of the personality.'

(op cit: p. 29)

Psycho-social development

Erikson, although considered by many clinicians to have contributed to the understanding of object–relations theory, nevertheless places unique emphasis on the importance of social development. According to Kernberg (1984), Erikson does not differentiate between the organization of self-representations and object-representations, and according to Jacobson (1964) he 'moves in a direction of a sociological conceptualisation of ego identity'.

Erikson's epigenetic chart places his eight own developmental stages alongside those of Freud:

(1)	Basic trust versus mistrust	0–1 years
(2)	Autonomy versus shame and doubt	1–3 years
(3)	Initiative versus guilt	3–5 years
(4)	Industry versus inferiority	6 years
(5)	Identity versus role confusion	adolescence
(6)	Intimate versus isolation	young/adulthood
(7)	Generativity versus stagnation	middle age
(8)	Ego integrity versus despair	old age

Erikson (1965) was interested in the conflicts and crises that arise when these stages do not flow easily into one another – as is frequently the case. It is important to note that although Erikson saw these stages as eight discrete steps, nevertheless he said they must all exist in some form or other from the beginning, as 'each comes to its ascendance, meets its crisis, and finds its lasting solution during the stage indicated'. Erikson claims that his analysis stands for all societies and for all people.

Anthropologists, myself included, would question the Western notion of imposing universality onto differing (especially non-Western) cultures.

Piaget's observation of intellectual development

Piaget's work has had a profound influence on both educationalists and psychologists (Piaget, 1962). Piaget repeatedly investigated how children adjust intellectually to the world in which they live and he identified four stages in the development of cognition:

(1) Sensorimotor   0–2 years
(2) Pre-operational   2–7 years
(3) Concrete operations 7–11 years
(4) Formal operations   11 years onwards

In terms of play, this represents an important move from stage 1 – which includes the discovery of the relationship between sensations and motor behaviour; 'object constancy' – knowing something exists when it cannot be seen – to stage 2 – which is the capacity to employ symbols, especially in language to portray the external world. Within this stage, Piaget claims that the child is egocentric, that is they can only grasp that their point of view is possible. Stage 3 is concerned with logic and maths and stage 4 with abstract thinking. Critics of Piaget suggest that he neglects feelings in this pursuit of intellect and pays little attention to the arts in contrast to science and maths. However, within its limitations in relation to childhood anxieties and dreams, it nevertheless forms an important aspect of the potential for the multi-model approach. According to Lahad (1992), for example, a child may be able to cope in the logical sphere of operations whereas they may not have coping skills in the affective areas. This would indicate that the logical sphere would form a basis for initial therapeutic work.

So far in this chapter, I have summarized, selectively and briefly, the work of theorists who put forward a developmental model of human psychology. I have included the object–relations of Freud, Klein and Winnicott, Jungian child analysis and sandplay, the psycho-social development of Erikson and the intellectual stages of Piaget.

2. DEVELOPMENTAL AND DRAMATIC PLAY

It is only relatively recently that our understanding of play and drama development has begun to be integrated into therapeutic approaches with children. Although writers whose work is described later in this chapter have been putting forward their ideas for many years, mainstream thinking has not yet been able to accommodate the relationship of the arts to play processes. This integrated model is described in more detail below. First, let us examine the contribution of play and drama practitioners to our understanding of playtherapy.

Slade (1954) published his seminal work, *Child Drama*, outlining a theory, methodology and practice for drama work with children and adolescents. His writing is constantly refreshing, especially when he talks about the *enjoyment* experienced by the child and uses terms such as:

'*Happiness-development*:   a stage in creative expression aimed at by the teacher. First signs of joy dependant on an out-flow.

Hinterland-activity: activity going on for love, in an absorbed fashion, generally out of view even when some other players are purposely in view. A natural development which takes place from time to time amongst children.

Out-flow: the pouring out of creative forms of expression, a tendency which can be regulated and encouraged, and which by frequent opportunity becomes a habit promoting confidence.'

Slade draws a major distinction between *personal play* in which the whole person or self is involved – what he calls 'obvious drama' which involves movement and characterization – and *projected play* where the main action takes place outside the body and is characterized by total absorption (see also the projective stage in Jennings' embodiment – projection – role paradigm 1987; 1990; 1992). Slade emphasizes the importance of personal play for social awareness and development. He is firm about not establishing fixed developmental categories though he draws our attention to the following:

'*0–3$\frac{1}{2}$ years*:   Peep-bo, sense trials (circle appears), art forms (including less obvious music and drama), the game, trials leading to play.

3$\frac{1}{2}$–4 years: Play proper and rhythm established (circle continues but properties abandoned).

5 years: Dramatic play.

6 years: The dawn of seriousness.

6$\frac{1}{2}$ years: The glorious years.

9 years: Plays created without aid (a further dawning of responsibility; the circle still continues).'

In 'the dawn of seriousness', Slade is referring to a frame of mind which becomes apparent at about six years of age and develops rapidly for the next four years or so. This manifests itself in the ability to discern good and evil, an awareness of society, and joy in work. Slade's concepts in *Child Drama* are original and have influenced the early beginnings of drama-in-education. (Slade was also the first person to put the two words drama and therapy together.)

Veronica Sherborne (1975; 1990) makes an important contribution to our understanding of the child's movement needs. I draw upon her ideas in the chapter that follows when I describe the embodiment stage of development. Sherborne pays attention to the fact that children should be able to experience their body *as a whole*, something which should precede the experience of individual body parts. These experiences can be re-created in playtherapy when they have not occurred in the first few months of life.

'The unconscious bodily experiences precede the development of the more conscious sense of identity in the child.'

(1975: p. 75)

Children should also be able to experience the centre of the body and thereby experience the continuity of movement flow through the body.

'Unco-ordinated and unself-aware children rarely experience a harmonious flow of movement through the different parts of the body.'

(*op cit*: p. 76)

Like other child specialists, Sherborne emphasizes the development of trust, something which is first experienced through the body – in holding and balancing for example. Here the child develops a trust of others as well as a trust of self. An extended part of Sherborne's work has been with children with profound learning difficulties, and there are several films available which illustrate her method. When working in playful movement, a key concept that she introduces is the notion of 'working with' and 'working against'; if a child is being rolled over and over, without resisting, then the child is working *with* the partner; if the child tries to resist being rolled then they are working *against* the partner. Sherborne suggests that too much emphasis on the former (working with) leads to the development of 'we' and group identity, and that it is important to allow resistance (working against) as an important component for developing the 'I' and individual identity.

Richard Courtney stresses that the stages he has observed in the dramatic development of the child do not apply cross-culturally. He was the major theorist after Slade to identify the earliest stages in play and drama and also to construct an analysis of different types of play.

'Thus drama provides the *felt* basis for rational thought.'

(Courtney, 1982: p. 17)

After the impersonatory stage of 0–10 months, Courtney marks what he calls 'The Primal Act' which occurs at about 10 months; the child acts 'as if' he is his mother, a manifestation which is founded on previous empathy, identification and imitation. Courtney considers that this primal act occurs in all cultures and is recognized in some as the time of the naming ceremony. It would seem that at the time of separation of identity, when the child is able to experience itself as other, he or she is then able to take the role of the other.

Courtney goes on to suggest that play activity can be divided as follows:

(1)   Symbolic play   1–2 years
(2)   Sequential play   2–3 years
(3)   Exploratory play   3–4 years
(4)   Expansive play   4–5 years
(5)   Flexible play   5–7 years

Although the above attributions are useful in understanding the child's expanding world of play, they should not be seen as exclusive or age-stage limited. All developmental categories, whether by orientation or observational theorists, may be seen as broad sweeps of a playful brush to enable us to understand the breadth as well as the depth of play activity and processes.

Courtney has also evolved a useful developmental checklist (see Appendix 1) as well as addressing the theme of assessment (Courtney & Schattner, 1981 pp. 5–20).

It should be added that there are numerous drama specialists who have written on dramatic play and work with young children and whose work is too extensive to mention here. Readers should, however, be aware of the work of Dorothy Heathcote, Gavin Bolton and Brian Way. These are but a few of the very special practitioners now working in this field, and I regard it as a privilege to have had the opportunity to work with the people who are mentioned in this section of the book.

3.   APPROACHES TO PLAY THERAPY

Most people who work with children acknowledge the innovatory work of Margaret Lowenfeld. Having trained as a doctor, some of her formative experiences were gathered in relief work in Poland after the war, where she recognized the resilience of children in stressful situations. In the introduction to the re-printing of her book *Introduction to Play in Childhood*, Davis (1991) describes how Lowenfeld paid attention to the pragmatic cognitive, somatic and affective elements of children, rather than to a theoretical or medical model.

> 'Though herself a charismatic character who attracted devoted disciples, Lowenfeld professed disbelief in the importance of transference in psychotherapy and put the emphasis on the children themselves being enabled to discover the positive aspects of their personalities. In this context she developed the so-called "World Technique" for exploring in a semi-structured fashion the important elements in a child's inner world by the way he or she arranged a set of representational toy figures in the landscape provided by the tray of sand.'
>
> (Davis, 1991: v)

Lowenfeld's writing demonstrates her detailed observation of children and play and her lists of materials (below), as well as the *variety* of materials that she insisted should be part of the therapist's equipment.

Fantasy material

> '*Inchoate*:   water and water toys, earth, sand, dough, modelling and paper-cutting materials, wood shapes and blocks, rods and holes.
>
> *Choate*:   "Worlds", mosaics, trains, grotesques, drawing, painting and acting materials.'

Additionally, she uses: 'construction materials, house or miniature adult material, and materials giving scope for movement and destruction.'

Lowenfeld goes on to say:

'Most easily procurable of the water toys are the rubber, celluloid, wood, and tin toys that can sink and float. Then come toy baths, bathrooms, and lavatories with working parts, kettles, teapots, cans from which water can be poured, soap-bubble pipes, water pistols and boats.

Sand and *Sand and Water* lend themselves to the demonstration of a large variety of phantasies, as, for example, tunnel-making, burying or drowning, land and seascapes. When wet, the same may be moulded, and when dry it is pleasant to feel, and many tactile experiments can be made with the gradual addition of moisture. Wet sand can be dried up again and reconverted to wet, or by adding further water it becomes "slosh", and finally water when the dry land has completely disappeared.'

(Lowenfeld, 1935: pp. 30 & 31)

Although a meticulous researcher into several play forms and materials, she is best known for the development of her 'World Technique' whereby a child is invited to create their world in the sandtray with any materials they choose. It may be the re-creation of an actual event that has happened, the expression of a fantasy, repetition over and over again of an important scene, and scenes that make complete sense to the child but are not understandable, even with description, to the therapist.

Such a playroom must have shelves full of all kinds of toys: animals, transport, human figures in occupations and in varying positions such as sitting and standing and natural objects such as twigs, stones and leaves.

Lowenfeld considers that the advantage of this type of material is that it allows, like a dream, two layers of meaning:

'1. on the surface is the manifest content, the actual scene which is represented.
2. by associative links between the items used to build up the scene, and the child's own past experience or interior life, ideas entirely different from those shown in the manifest content can be expressed.'

(*op cit*: p. 114)

Lowenfeld also considers that it is important for specialists to be properly trained because of the powerful nature of the medium they are using.

As mentioned above, the Jungian sandplay therapists, most notably Dora Kalff, have been influenced by the Lowenfeld approach. Kalff describes the importance of having a variety of materials and, like Lowenfeld, emphasizes the size of the sandbox: it should be the right size for the eye to encompass, and it creates a space which she describes as both *free* and *protected*.

'The child has absolute freedom in determining what to construct, which figures to choose and how to use them. The same limitations that are prerequisite for genuine freedom in the real world, are present in the measurements of the sandbox, which are scaled down to man's size, thereby setting up limits as to what can be represented and providing a frame wherein the transformation can take place.'

(*op cit*: p. 39)

Virginia Axline's book *Dibs in Search of Self* describes in detail the process of non-directive play therapy with a single child client. Her textbook, *Play Therapy*, now reprinted, makes a useful introduction to her specific non-directive approach. Axline's approach is to reflect back to the child what he or she (and sometimes they as she also does group play therapy) says. From time to time she offers interpretation based on the here and now and not on past history. She stresses the individuality of all children and the importance of total acceptance of, and respect for, the child whatever he or she may offer. She does not believe in diagnostic interviews before therapy commences and bases her approach on always starting where the child is. She believes that too many people attempt to exploit a child's personality, and that this is why identities are so strongly defended.

'During a play-therapy experience, that sort of relationship is established between the therapist and the child that makes it possible for the child to reveal his real self to the therapist, and, having had it accepted – and, by that very acceptance, having grown a bit in self-confidence – he is able to extend the frontiers of his personality expression.'

(Axline, 1969: p. 23)

Axline warns that play therapy is not an imposition of desirable standards by adults onto children, and often children that come to her for play therapy do not know they have problems. She maintains her non-directive stance in the way she describes that the play of the child is child-centred and is what the child wants to do:

'The therapist renders unto the child what is the child's – in this case the toys and the undirected use of them. When he plays freely and without direction, he is expressing his personality. He is experiencing a period of independent thought and action. He is releasing the feelings and attitudes that have been pushing to get out into the open.'

(*op cit*: p. 22)

Axline's book is well illustrated with detailed case history transcripts and she also describes the basic resources needed by play therapists. There is much that I support in her work, in particular her respect of the child and the child-centred approach. Whereas she supports the non-directive approach, I believe that the playtherapist can establish a relationship with the child *through the play* – can enter into the play world – and that this may provide structure, without being directive.

Violet Oaklander's (1978) approach presents a contrast to that of Axline: she has evolved a series of specific techniques which she had found 'work' for her clients and herself. She says in *Windows to Our Children* that whatever activity she engages in with a child, the basic purpose of the sessions is always as follows:

'My goal is to help the child become aware of herself and her existence in the world. Each therapist will find his or her own style in achieving that delicate balance between directing and guiding the session on the one hand, and going with and following the child's lead on the other.'

(Oaklander, 1978: p. 53)

Oaklander frequently uses drawing as a starting point, something which establishes self-identity as well as allowing the expression of feelings. She suggests several stages of how a session could then develop through the many different ways in which the picture can be shared: sharing the experience of creating the picture; asking the child to tell the story of the picture; maybe leading into an elaboration in more detail; 'role-reversing' with the picture; encouraging the child to go further with a description by asking non-invasive questions – 'where is she going?', for example. She emphasizes the importance of watching for cues in the child's voice-tone, body-posture, facial and body expression, breathing, silence:

'Silence can mean censoring, thinking, remembering, repression, anxiety, fear, or awareness of something'.

(*op cit*: p. 54)

Like Slade and Sherborne quoted above, Oaklander uses the term 'flow' when she says that therapists should use the child's non-verbal cues to promote a flow in their work. She continues to work with pictures and stories to assist the child where possible to own what belongs to them and move on from the situation. She points out that therapy can be brief and deal with a specific dynamic.

One of Oaklander's well-known methods is the rosebush fantasy. She asks children to close their eyes, go into their own space and then imagine that they are rosebushes. She gives lots of prompting, with questions such as:

> '"What sort of a rosebush are you?"
> "Are you very small?"
> "Are you very large?" "Do you have flowers?" (they don't have to be roses)
> and so on, creating a wealth of permission for the child to freely enter the fantasy. The child tells the story of the rosebush or describes the rosebush in the first person (role-reversal). A client of mine was able to express her concerns about her family dying when she drew the rosebush and said:

> "I am trying to grow strong as there won't be a gardener to look after me in the rose garden."'

Oaklander also uses multi-media and the importance of the therapist's creative use of self.

4.   THE PLAYTHERAPY METHOD

In section 1 of this chapter I considered contrasting developmental models of child analysis, play and intellectual development. In section 2, particular attention was paid to the contribution of those working with drama and children. The third section outlined three major contributions to the history and development of playtherapy. Although I have tried to include major influences throughout this chapter, these cannot represent either a complete overview or history of play and therapy. Inevitably they are compiled from the sources that have influenced me in my own work during its emergence over the last three decades. Just as in the Introduction, where I described the childhood and early adult experiences that have shaped who *I* am, this chapter illustrates the many formative influences in the world of clinical and dramatic theory and play therapy that have guided, inspired and also provoked me.

During these years I have evolved what I call the Playtherapy Method, which forms the basis for the subsequent chapters in this book. It can be used in short-, medium- and long-term intervention with children and adolescents. It has been substantially influenced by my dramatherapy work with children and the very early ideas I developed in my first book *Remedial Drama* (1973). It does not rely on analysis and interpretation by adults to children. While not disregarding psychoanalytic thinking, the Playtherapy Method regards this form of observation as one dimension of the child's world which at times takes on its own mythic qualities. For example, to perceive the small infant as monstrous because it bites the breast is an adult projection, that is a way of talking about an adult opinion, and my concern with some psychoanalytic writing is that assumptions are made about child behaviour which carry with them very emotional loading on the one hand and pseudo-scientific language on the other. I suppose it is taking an enormous step for me to challenge the traditional order of child analysis and I must state that I have been reassured in my view by the recent writings of Alice Miller.

However, I do want to stress that I do not feel it is an *either or* situation – my difficulty with so much analytic writing is that it is exclusive and narrow in its frame of reference.

As we have seen from the various writings above, there are parallel and interweaving theories on child and play development. My concern is that we should not take an exclusive view of children's playing and fit it into one theoretical stance. A rigid frame *oversimplifies and reduces* the child's world; my belief is that our intervention should be able to *contain and expand* the child's world.

The creative imagination

The infant is born with creative potential and the capacity to symbolize: indeed, it is the very capacity of human beings to pretend or make-believe which enables them to survive. We cannot envisage a life within which we could not imagine how things are – how they were, or how they might be. The creative imagination is the most important attribute that we can foster in children, and it is the basis of creative playfulness.

Proto-play

During the first year of life, infants are reacting and responding to the world around them; the warmth and symbiosis of the first few weeks gives way to increasing curiosity and experimentation. There is an emphasis on sensory experience and bodily security and exploration; a growing awareness of the known pleasure and excitement and the unknown 'surprise' which can give rise either to a laughter or a fear response. In the second six months, there is clear emergence of the child as actor – pretends to be mother ('primal' act, see above) – and responds to audience; pretending, repetition, seen and unseen (such as in the game of peep-bo).

Before the age of one year we can observe the child move *from mimicry* (above) *to impersonation*. Although there is repetition of sounds, movements, words and so on, there is a delight in the new, the different and the unexpected. The child is responding to and instigating the most basic constellation of *ritual and risk*.

Transitionary time

Towards the end of the first twelve months and onwards, the child makes use of a range of media in explorations of self and the world. Winnicott refers to the *transitional object* – often a blanket or soft piece of cloth which the child will carry around and talk with. Again we see the ritual/risk paradigm: the object must stay the same and not be washed or replaced, but it becomes a vehicle for increased imaginative risk-taking. It is named, talked with, and the infant answers on its behalf, i.e. role-reverses. The transitional object, and other transitionary phenomena – special toys, treasures, clothes – enable the child to move from the concrete to the symbolic, to enter the world of imaginative play.

Play and proto-art

The child is now in the world of 'let's pretend': toys can be characters; things are used as toys; 'seen and not seen' develops in games, nest, den and house-building. There is an extension of sensory play – sand and water, finger paint, clay and Plasticine – which later becomes crayoning and brush painting, a mixture of projective play and personal play (see Slade, above). The child develops as actor, dancer, director, script-writer, scenic designer, and will move from one activity to another and one role to another.

The child knows when it is involved in an activity – sometimes for its own sake – and when it is in role 'doing' an activity. *Once a child is in a role or character, doing something, it has entered the world of dramatic play and drama.*

The child develops an increasing aesthetic sense – it is now in the world of art. Here the imagination can be creative and can refine the creation – things are perfected and tried again; alternatives are experimented with and choices made; and certain experiences are returned to – favourite dramas, stories, characters.

Thus the child moves through different constellations of proto-play, transitionary media, play, proto-art, dramatic play and dramatic art all of which are influenced by the cultural and familial context within which the child grows up. I do not intend to put rigid age stages on these activities, nor to suggest that they are unilinear: spiral experience and learning are of a fundamental importance when looking at the creative act. In other words, one returns with the spiral but to a different place and one may spiral down or spiral up; in addition, the spiral may close in and focus or may branch out and flourish. The following developmental paradigm of the Playtherapy Method gives broad categories within its three stages.

The developmental paradigm Embodiment–Projection–Role (EPR)

Embodiment: Most prominent during the first year of life. Sensory experience, holding, whole body and parts.

Projection: Experiences are projected out into various toys and media. Media (e.g. sand and water) also heighten the sensory experience. Toys take on roles and relationships and child controls outcome.

Role: Child takes on the role or the character and moves into different roles; integrates activity with role and creates the story or directs the drama.

The developmental paradigm may be used as an assessment tool to see where the child wishes to start. This may be with the picture

(Oaklander) and then into dramatic play or it may be with the body (Sherborne) and then projection and role.

It is important, however, that all children are able to navigate these stages in play and in playtherapy if they have not had this primary experience in their first years of life.

I wish to close this chapter with a reminder of why it has been written in the first place: in order to assist adults to assist children. I am reminded of the theatre director Peter Brook's use of the French word 'assistance' in his creative paradigm for the actor: répétition–représentation–assistance

Répétition that the actor needs – the drudge that will bring about change – 'harnessed to an aim, driven by a will, répétition is creative' (Brook, 1968).

Représentation – the French word for performance – meaning when something is re-presented; it is not an imitation of a past event but a *making present* which has immediacy.

Assistance – again from the French word for watching a play (j'assiste à une pièce – Brook, *op cit*); the transformation that happens between actor and audience comes from the assistance of the audience – they are no longer divided from the actor by the représentation.

In the playtherapy I have shared with children, I have discovered, paradoxically, so much about reality – both my own and the child's. I hope the ensuing chapters will assist you into the playtherapy methods that I have found creative in my own worlds.

REFERENCES

Axline, V. (1964) *Dibs in Search of Self*. London: Penguin.
Axline, V. (1969) *Play Therapy*. Revised edition. New York: Ballentine Books.
Brook, P. (1968) *The Empty Space*. London: Penguin Books.
Courtney, R. (1982) *Re-Play*. Toronto: OISE Press.
Courtney, R. & Schattner, G. (1981) *Drama in Therapy*, Vol. 1 'Children'. New York: Drama Book Specialists.
Davis, J. (1991) Introduction to *Play in Childhood* by M. Lowenfeld. London: MacKeith Press.
Erikson, E. (1965) *Childhood and Society*. Harmondsworth: Penguin.

Fordham, M. (1986) *Jungian Psychotherapy*. London: Maresfield.

Jacobson, E. (1964) *The Self and the Object World*. New York: International Universities Press.

Jennings, S. (1973) *Remedial Drama*. London: A & C Black.

Jennings, S. (1987) *Dramatherapy Theory and Practice*. London: Routledge.

Jennings, S. (1990) *Dramatherapy with Families, Groups and Individuals*. London: Jessica Kingsley.

Jennings, S. (Ed) (1992) *Dramatherapy Theory and Practice 2*. London: Routledge.

Jung, C.G. (1967) *Memories, Dreams, Reflections*. London: Routledge.

Kalff, D.M. (1980) *Sandplay*. Santa Monica, Ca: Sigo Press.

Kernberg, O. (1984) *Object-Relations Theory and Clinical Psychoanalysis*. New York: Jason Aronson.

Lahad, M. (1992) Story-making in assessment methods for coping with stress: six-piece story-making and BASIC Ph. In *Dramatherapy Theory and Practice 2* (Ed. S. Jennings). London: Routledge.

Landy, R. (1986) *Drama Therapy*. Chicago, Illinois: Charles C. Thomas.

Lowenfeld, M. (1935) *Play in Childhood*. London: MacKeith Press.

Neumann, E. (1973) *The Child*. London: Hodder and Stoughton.

Oaklander, V. (1978) *Windows to our Children*. Moab, Utah: Real People Press.

Piaget, J. (1962) *Play, Dreams and Imitation in Childhood*. London: Routledge.

Rycroft, C. (1985) *Psychoanalysis and Beyond*. London: Chatto & Windus.

Sherborne, V. (1975) 'Movement for retarded and disabled children'. In *Creative Therapy* (Ed. Sue Jennings). Banbury: Kemble Press.

Sherborne, V. (1990) *Developmental Movement for Children*. Cambridge: Cambridge University Press.

Slade, P. (1954) *Child Drama*. London: University of London Press.

Winnicott, D. (1975) *Through Paediatrics to Psychoanalysis*. London: Hogarth Press.

Chapter 2

Embodiment and Sensory Play

Can you keep a secret?
I don't suppose you can,
You mustn't laugh or giggle
While I tickle your hand.[1]

Iona and Peter Opie, 1959

STAGE 1: EMBODIMENT

In this chapter I describe embodiment, stage 1 of the developmental paradigm of embodiment–projection–role (EPR). I have included the words 'sensory play' in the title because it forms such an important part of the embodiment stage. Although we refer to the embodiment stage as taking place during the first year of life, it is possible to re-experience it, even as an adult, through careful therapeutic intervention.

The body and its relationship with other bodies – through touch and the other senses – forms the basis for the development of identity in all human beings. However it is important to remember that our identity depends on the *relationship* between bodies, not only on touch and senses; therefore there needs to be a balance between touch and separation, between the we and the I (see Chapter 1).

THE DEVELOPING BODY-SELF

The human body represents a *primary* means of learning. From birth, the human infant continuously receives experiences through the body in relation to other people and the environment. *It is through these early experiences that an infant develops a body-self which is necessary before the development of a body image.*

The body-self can only develop in a fulsome sense through contact with other body-self(s) – usually the adult carer and, most frequently, the mother. During the first few weeks of life, most

25

physical contact is through nurturing and caring actions such as holding, feeding, changing, washing, rocking, and dressing.

Clothes themselves can provide additional warmth and nurture: notice how young and old alike prefer flannelette and Wincyette for night clothes and bedding. Recently, it has been realized that premature babies will thrive if placed on lambskin rather than on cotton sheets.

Gradually, more stimulating contact begins as the carer uses different forms of touch; varies vocal sounds; talks to and answers on behalf of the child. Most parents carry on a dialogue with the child which the child soon tries to imitate in sounds and gestures.

It is worth noting here how often we have dialogues either with ourselves or with people and animals who cannot possibly reply. This is an important aspect of role and character development and will be discussed more fully in Chapter 4.

Early in the first year, the infant achieves a major physical land-mark, that of being able to roll over unaided (sometimes getting stuck in the process). This is the first time that the infant has managed the whole of its body unaided and has literally turned its world upside-down. Other major body stages follow:

- *Sitting unaided* (encouraged and assisted by adults)
- *Crawling* – using just hands, then hands and knees, and hands and feet (crawling is not always encouraged by adults)
- *Walking* (first assisted by others and then independently)

During this time, the child's senses are being stimulated and in turn explored. Smell, for example, is the oldest sense and it is suggested that the child's sense of smell (in that it belongs to the oldest area of the brain) helps it to differentiate its biological mother. The child also quickly recognizes the familiar sounds from the mother and gradually takes an interest in new and unfamiliar sounds. The infant is both touched itself and is able to explore the touch of people and objects in the immediate surroundings. Its sense of sight is stimulated when it recognizes familiar faces and follows moving objects. Taste as a sense receives less stimulation in the first year and remains a relatively bland sense until later in the child's development; the infant does, however, use the mouth for touch exploration.

The expanding world

From this initial world of nurture, the child's world then begins to expand in the following ways:

- Physical exploration of immediate surroundings
- Stimulation of the child with a variety of sensation
- The child being carried from place to place
- The increased mobility of the child
- The child's increasing range of vocal sounds
- The child's world being peopled by others

Moreover, this expansion, according to Catherine Garvey (1977: p. 30), also involves the infant.

> 'Not even in the first four months, however, does an infant receive playful adult attention *passively*. Entertainment through motion and sensation may be offered by parents, but the infant takes part. The early play of an infant and its parent has an intrinsic goal that Daniel Stern has described as "pure inter-action". The means by which parents can create and maintain an optimal level of attention and arousal in an infant (whose obvious signals of pleasure further promote their efforts) consist of sounds, facial expressions and movements, often including physical contact.'

It is important in relation to children's play and later artistic development to recognize pre-play activity that starts before a child can walk independently. Before a child is physically mobile, it is able to accomplish the following actions:

- Make sounds in rhythm
- Make movements in rhythm
- Make marks
- Imitate sounds and facial expressions

The making of rhythmic sounds and movement needs no further explanation. Mark-making is generally discouraged by parents – particularly in societies where there is an emphasis on children being clean and not messy or sticky. However, if we observe the small infant, we can see the pleasure derived from mark-making with food and, if given the opportunity, with feces. The mark-making is related to the exploration of texture and substance; we can also see this in the pleasures of dribbling, saliva bubble-blowing, and the discovery of all exits and entrances to the body.

The child's early sounds are usually imitations of adult sounds, and this consists not only of sound, but of the expression and intonation that accompanies it. Parents are often taken aback to hear their own sound-patterns being voiced back to them, and gradually, as children differentiate facial expressions and gestures, these are mirrored too.

We can see in this early *sounding, moving, mark-making* and *imitation*, activities which I call *proto-play*, the early manifestation of what will later become music, dance, art and drama: that is, the arts. How these will develop will depend on the familial and cultural influences surrounding the child. It should also be noted here that not all cultures differentiate between art-forms as we do; some may have a single word for the activity or even refer to it as play. Since I see play as a necessary stage for the development of what we choose to call 'art', I still refer to this earlier activity as proto-play.

Proto-play forms a major part of the embodiment stage of development and emerges through satisfactory experiences of being held and stimulated together with sufficient nurture. Proto-play continues to develop as the adult *engages* with the child (otherwise the child will develop only isolated play) and most of the early engagement is via the body – whether through touch, sound or facial expression. Adults who feel uncomfortable with their own body identity may have problems in physical communication with children. Therefore it is essential for playtherapists to have a good understanding and training of their own bodies.

Furthermore, if adults are unable to 'read' the bodily signals from the child and are not at ease with their own bodies, then a range of problematic situations can develop.

THE UNDER-, OVER- AND DISTORTEDLY-HELD CHILD

When children are what I refer to as *under-held, over-held* or *distortedly-held*, they will not flourish and may develop severe impairment.

The under-held child

The under-held child is:

- Neglected
- Left alone for long periods
- Not stimulated

- Not affirmed
- Often fails to thrive
- May become non-responsive and lethargic

The child who is not held enough develops neither a sense of security and support nor a sense of *body-self*. A child needs to experience its body-self before it can develop a body-image.

The following extended case history serves as an example of a situation where the child's early experience was severely impoverished:

Case history

I was asked to do a home visit to assess a child for a 'special nursery' which had been established for those children thought to be at risk in terms of development. The nursery accepted a wide variety of children, including those with a mental handicap, physical disability, speech, sight, or hearing impairment, delicate children, as well as children having difficulty in making a transition from home to nursery. We accepted children from nine months to four years who were referred from education, health visitors, GPs or social services.

Bobby, aged two, had been referred by his health visitor who was worried about his development; it turned out that there had also been an enquiry from the parents concerning finding foster parents for him as they considered him handicapped. While the situation was being considered, it was thought that the special nursery could provide some relief for the parents, as well as some stimulus for the child.

When I arrived to visit the family, his mother was very anxious and wanted to tell me everything that they had done in order to be good parents. The house was spotless and I was offered a cup of coffee. Afterwards the cup was immediately seized and washed up. It was difficult to get the mother to sit and relax while she talked with me. Her story seemed very sad. She and her husband had met through their work in computing and had started playing squash together regularly. They had similar interests in work and sport and so had married, thinking that one day a baby might be a nice idea.

The baby arrived after two years, and, the mother went on to say,

'that's when all the problems started. We never thought having a boby would create such a terrible problem. It has really ruined our lives – and we had a good life. It doesn't seem fair. I think the whole idea of having babies is pretty disgusting anyway. I asked the doctor if I could have a full anaesthetic so I didn't know what was happening. He said they would only do that if it was a Caesarian and that might be the case since I have small hips – so I was banking on that. And David and I agreed that he should wait at home till it was all over: I didn't want him to see me in any sort of mess. Anyway, I had the operation, so didn't come round until I had the stitches and everything done, and one underweight bundle was put into my lap. Of course I didn't want to feed, so there was all the routine of the bottles and mixing and everything. The nurses did it in the hospital and then I had to do it when they sent me home a week later. They kept saying he had to put on weight, so I had to keep feeding him all times of the night and day. I tried to get him on a routine, but I couldn't stand the crying. Whenever he cries, I just stick something in his mouth. I've been at home with him all this time, just clearing up and washing and bathing. It's a full-time job, and I don't like it. I want to go back to work: I want to play squash again with my husband. I'm worried that my figure has gone to seed now that I'm not exercising. He still goes, and there are plenty of young trim women at the club. And I'm terrified of having another baby – so every month I get anxious.'

As she told me this in an almost non-stop monologue, she sat there screwing a handkerchief around her fingers and fighting hard to keep her tears back. She did not appear to have 'gone to seed' and indeed looked immaculate. I felt that it was not the place to explore the various levels of what she was saying (gone to seed?), but I also felt that she and her husband needed some help. I said that I should see Bobby and then we could have a chat about possible options she and her husband might like to consider.

She led me to a space at the foot of the stairs – a space about four feet square that had been fenced off, with guard-rails in the doorway to any rooms and to the stairs. There was polythene lining the floor and a blue blanket placed over it. Bobby was sitting in a corner, totally placid, sucking a thumb. His mother immediately removed his thumb from his mouth, saying, 'I've told you before – stop that!' Inside the 'cage' were three balloons, a small teddy-bear, and a cushion. Bobby was overweight and continued to sit throughout.

When I asked if Bobby could walk yet, she replied that that was why they had realized he was handicapped, because he could not walk, feed himself, or do anything for himself, and he was not clean or dry. I asked if we could take him out of the play-pen and she fetched me a 'pinny' to keep my clothes clean; she then lifted him up, holding him at a distance, and passed him to me. We returned to the kitchen and sat down. Bobby sat still on my lap, looked at his mother and put a hand out, saying 'urhh, urhh'. She said 'that means he wants a drink. Keep him for a moment while I sort things out'. She brought a high chair with a harness out of the cupboard, put Bobby into it, tied a full-length bib onto him, and proceeded to give him a drink from a beaker with a spout while she held his arms away. The telephone rang and she went to answer it whereupon the child promptly grasped the beaker for himself and started to drink: there was no problem of his knowing what to do.

When she returned, I suggested that Bobby started at the nursery three mornings a week; that he would be fetched and brought back; and would she send some play-clothes in case the children got messy. She winced at this, but said she would like him to attend while they were exploring the possibility of fostering.

Bobby started at the nursery the following week, and arrived with a brand new set of overalls for messy play. He was quite overwhelmed by the level of noise and people, and we allotted one of the workers to be with him all the time and to gradually introduce him to the various activities. After a couple of weeks, he was assessed and found to have normal intelligence, but to be functioning at roughly the level of an eighteen-month-old due to understimulation and *lack of physical bonding*.

His parents did manage to have him fostered, and eventually he was adopted into a family with two children who were very boisterous and physical. He continued at the nursery where he progressed through a developmental programme of movement and play where the early stages of embodiment were re-experienced. The foster-parents were involved in the whole programme, reinforcing the work at the nursery. Bobby was allowed to regress in his movement with constant rocking and cradling; games with rolling, pulling and pushing across the floor; building shelters with people, and being able to climb and explore. He soon pulled himself up to a walking position and walked independently within three months.

Bobby's speech was very slow to develop and he tried to get everything he wanted by making noises and pointing. The staff quickly realized that this behaviour was inhibiting further speech. They designed a play programme for all the children which involved a range of sounds and use of the breath. The important thing to note here is that, with Bobby, it was important to start from the *early* bodily stages, those that Bobby had not experienced in his family.

(Although Bobby's parents were offered the support of marital therapy, they declined, saying that everything was fine now that Bobby was in a foster home. They readily agreed to his adoption, and did not have any more children: in fact his mother told the health visitor that she was waiting for sterilization.)

Teaching point

As can be seen from the above example, this child's development was seriously affected by the lack of physical contact with adults, and, additionally, by the lack of stimulation both from parents and from the environment – in his case what I call a 'soft' environment. (There will be further discussion on play environments in Chapter 9.)

I give this as an example of the child who is *under-held*. Deprived of physical contact, the child does not develop a sense of body-self or the ability to achieve normal landmarks in physical mastery. In fact, infants who are not held usually become lethargic and depressed, a state that is mistaken by many parents as 'being good'.

The over-held child

The child who is over-held is:

- Over-protected
- Not stimulated
- Not encouraged to risk-take
- Has difficulty becoming independent
- Is often frightened of exploring

This state may occur when there has been difficulty at birth, or difficulty in conceiving in the first place, or if a child is premature, ill or disabled. Sometimes the child still represents the 'dream baby' – becoming what the parents have longed for – and is smothered with care and attention like a love object rather than being encouraged as an individual in its own right. The smothering love is different from the holding, nurturing and exploration of touch that *all children need*. All children need additional *holding*, where the child is just held, stroked and massaged, quite apart from the holding involved in attending to the bodily needs of feeding and cleaning.

If parents have difficulties during the conception stage (Jennings, 1992) and the resultant child has arrived after lengthy treatments and periods of waiting, it can be difficult for them to allow the child to develop autonomy. An example which illustrates this is of the parents who woke up every two hours in order to check that their child was still breathing.

It is not easy for any parent to gauge the appropriate balance between nurture and independence. Nurture consists not only of the response to bodily functions such as feeding and cleaning but also the *emotional* need to be held, massaged and stroked. It is this very way of holding that becomes smothering when the parent is doing it for their own needs rather than the needs of the child. Once again there needs to be a balance because, obviously, parents have needs too, and one way they are satisfied is in engagement with the child.

An extreme example of over-holding can be illustrated by the practice of wrapping small babies in tight swaddling clothes; although these provide close containment on the one hand, they allow absolutely no bodily movement on the other.

Case history

'Screaming Charlie' is a good example of the over-held child – the child's nickname was given to him by neighbours and relatives when Charlie, aged two, was allowed to scream for whatever he wanted until it was given to him.

Charlie was conceived after a series of miscarriages over a five-year period. His mother was ordered bed-rest – yet again – when she conceived for the sixth time. Although there were some signs of bleeding, this time the pregnancy continued and Charlie was born, six weeks prematurely, and spent his first two weeks in an incubator. His mother stayed at the hospital day and night and when she took Charlie home, he became the entire focus of her life. Not only did he have very frequent medical check-ups and second opinions, but he was never allowed out of his mother's sight.

Her husband coped for a few months but soon drifted away into a more immediate relationship when he was no longer able to engage with his wife or, indeed, have relaxed access with his son. Without her husband as a mediating factor, Charlie's mother was able to devote even more time to the beloved child and he grew up in an atmosphere of total attention, sterilized food and toys, and a hovering anxiety that something might be wrong.

The family's GP suggested that Charlie might benefit from nursery school and, after much reluctance, his mother allowed him to try; however, the staff eventually had to ask her to leave with her son because she would not stay away herself and cross-examined the staff on their hygiene, food, and so on. Charlie had not yet developed socially at all and was unable to engage in playing. He was eventually referred by the GP for psychological assessment after the teacher at his primary school said he was still functioning at the level of a two-year-old. Charlie was referred for playtherapy but it was quickly realized that the most important thing was to get appropriate referral for his mother. She did enter psychotherapy and went through a period of playtherapy herself in order to help him make the bridges into more mature ways of behaving.

> ***Teaching point***
>
> Without wishing to enter the one-parent/two-parent debate, in this situation it seems clear that Charlie's father may well have been a mediating factor and even have helped to bring about change if early enough support could have been obtained for the family as a whole.
>
> In such a situation one can only welcome the enlightened insistence of the GP – otherwise Charlie could well have ended up in long-term therapy for a situation that needed his mother to change. Charlie was later helped to handle his need for independence in a realistic way. The screaming bouts ceased to occur after the first therapy session.

Children who are neither over- nor under-held

The following example (Jennings, 1992) illustrates how physical holding of itself does not impede maturation and independence. The Senoi Temiar people live in the tropical rain-forest of Malaysia; both men and women give time and attention to the early years of children, and especially to the first few months. All babies are massaged from birth, both by the mother and the midwife, for several weeks. The women warm their hands by the fire and then press each limb, firmly and repeatedly, outlining the shape of the child's body. They pay special attention to the head, and the midwife deliberately closes up the fontanelle and re-shapes the head if there is any distortion from the birth. Infants are breast-fed on demand for several years, and spend most of their first year on the hip or back of mother, grandmother, father, or teenage sibling.

Temiar children walk earlier than their Western counterparts and have finer motor-control and balance. In this context it is interesting to note that Temiar mothers discourage crawling and encourage children to stand and walk as early as possible. Even from a few weeks of age, mothers let infants grasp their fingers and then gently pull them to their feet.

Distorted-holding

Let us now consider the child who has been inappropriately or violently held – the more extreme versions of the under- or over-held child. There is a section in Chapter 8 discussing work with children who are abused, and there is also further information about working with violence in later chapters. Here, I wish to set out some guidelines for body-play when physical abuse is suspected or proven.

Some workers feel uncomfortable with the idea of body play with children who have suffered body trauma. They often in fact focus on the telling of what happened rather than on the repair and re-parenting that is necessary.

'The scorn and abuse directed at the helpless child as well as the suppression of vitality, creativity, and feeling in the child and in oneself permeate so many areas of our life that we hardly notice it anymore. Almost everywhere we find the effort, marked by varying degrees of intensity and by the use of various coercive measures, to rid ourselves as quickly as possible of the child within us – i.e. the weak, helpless, dependent creature – in order to become an independent, competent adult deserving of respect.'

Alice Miller, 1981

Although the results of over-, or under-holding may be compensated for and redressed later in life, distorted embodiment experiences often take much longer to treat and may cause permanent damage if the problem is not diagnosed in childhood. The following are examples of distorted-holding:

- Physical abuse, i.e. blows
- Sexual abuse – exploration and/or penetration
- Physical neglect
- Lack of safety, e.g. dropping the child
- Distorted feeding

In small infants, such holding often does not come to light unless there is non-accidental injury or it has been noticed that the child does not thrive. The worst types of cases often end with the death of a child and/or a Court case. However, it may be that a child does survive and is treated, when he or she is older, in therapy. Although such distortions may permanently damage a child, recall before the age of two years is rare in most children.

Often the emphasis in treatment is too much on attempted disclosure rather than the repair and re-parenting that is needed to provide a nurturing embodiment experience. Work with the body is important to re-establish touch, trust, and later creativity. This process may take a long time and, for the child who has suffered undue violence, requires working and waiting with patience.

> ### Teaching point
>
> Frequently such a child needs more personal space – that is the space that surrounds him or her – and as workers we need to be sensitive to this and gauge the proximity to another human being that the child can tolerate. The space between child and adult can be bridged through the use of woven materials – long strips of chiffon, for example, that can help establish contact without being invasive.
>
> Safety can also be established by allowing the child to create a 'home base' with a large hoop, play-mat or large cushion. This creation of the 'larger space' to institute a layer of protection can be compared to the obese person who creates a similar safety layer, using their own body.

Ultimately the aim of all interventions is to assist the child to re-experience nurturing and boisterous play as safe occupations that can be enjoyed without fear of violence. The child may also need to play through the violence he or she has actually experienced and there are many different ways of doing this. These will be discussed further in Chapters 6 and 8.

REPAIR AND REPARENTING

In the case of the over-held child, he or she is likely to be very dependent as well as to have problems separating from the mother. Such a child will also be understimulated in terms of the expanding world and have a fear of exploration and risk.

The under-held child will not have experienced primary nurturing and is likely to be depressed, lethargic and without a developed body-self. If the child is stimulated out of its lethargy, it may well be anxious, nervous, hyperactive, clumsy and have lack of attention-span.

The child who has experienced distorted-holding will have a chaotic experience of his or her own body and no sense of body-self.

The start of the playtherapy process

Finding bodily starting points is important with all these children: over-held children need to start from their own point of security and move further on and the under-held child needs to re-trace the various bodily stages. This is most effectively achieved by means of *body-play*. (This is also applicable for adults who have missed out on their own early play experiences.)

The following body-play ideas, although designed for work in groups, may be easily adapted for one-to-one work. It is possible to do a lot of one-to-one work within groups as well if you have available a team of volunteers or school-leavers so that each child has an adult carer (see also the training staff section in Chapter 10). The movements used include the normal developmental stages of human infants and, additionally, become the basis of interaction, both working *with* a person and working *against* a person (Earlier in the book I paid tribute to Veronica Sherborne whose pioneering work in this field is a source of inspiration.)

It is important to remember that the movements described do not become just exercises; they are part of playing. The chapter ends on three dramatized playtherapy scenes which show how playful learning and re-learning and re-learning can be achieved, while at the same time incorporating essential bodily stages.

EMBODIMENT METHODS

Rolling

This involves free rolling into the centre of the room and out again (see Fig. 2.1). Groups can roll over each other and thereby develop trust and confidence.

- Rolling in pairs – one person is a log and the other rolls them; the log then becomes stuck and the person has to use a lot of effort to shift it (i.e. rolling with the partner, resisting being rolled and working against).
- Rolling in jelly – one person is floppy with no resistance and the partner tries to roll them.
- Rolling an adult – several children try to roll an adult and test their strength and confidence.

Rolling is a very safe activity that is exploratory in nature. A floor is supportive – you cannot fall off a floor – and it gives constant

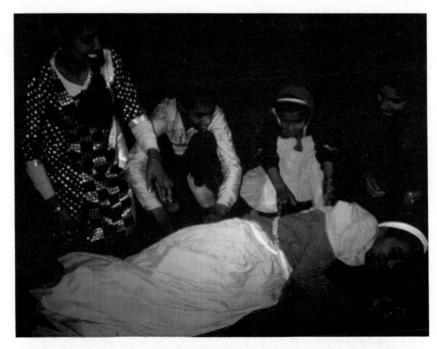

Fig. 2.1   Embodiment: two children rolling one adult.

feedback to the shape and weight of one's body; in addition, no one is too heavy to roll. Rolling also stimulates perception as the world changes around you, while rolling in pairs develops social interaction and tests limits.

Teaching point

It is important not to allow a collective and inclusive *we* – as in 'we will all do this' – to develop, otherwise the experience becomes a limited one of collective and co-operative endeavour. Children also need to be able to differentiate a healthy *I* in order to reinforce individual identity. This sense of identity is encouraged through resistance-movements.

It should be noted that it is also important for a child who is compliant and dependent to be able to say 'no' with their bodies. This is obviously important when working with children who have suffered physical abuse and this is discussed later in the chapter.

Fig. 2.2 Embodiment: a young boy is trying to pull his partner across the room.

Whole-body floor movements

- Hold partner by the ankles and give them a ride (Fig. 2.2). Make 'patterns' by sliding the person from side-to-side.
- Partner lies on side and draws up knees to chin. Partner unfolds them and folds them up again.
- Person lies on front and pulls him- or herself along by hands and arms. Lying on back and propelling oneself by legs.

- Person lies in a star-shape (on back), arms and legs outstretched. Partners dance over the limbs like a sword-dance (a high-risk exercise, not to be attempted in early stages).
- Person lies in a star-shape (on front) and imagines they are stuck to floor. Partner has to unstick them.

Sitting

- Sitting in pairs, back-to-back, feeling another person's back against your own. Give partner a ride by pushing their back and then resist being pushed – quite literally, this teaches a child 'not to be pushed around'.
- Sitting in threes, one behind the other; all move together. Become a boat and sail on the sea.
- Sitting in pairs, holding hands. Third person tries to 'get in'. Vary it with one person trying to 'get out'.

Crawling

- Crawling around room on hands and knees; crawling over or under other people in the room.
- Half the group make bridges for the others to crawl under.
- Two people (then three, four, and more) make a bridge for others to crawl under. Repeat for people to crawl over.

Trust exercise

Several people place themselves side-by-side in the crawl position. Another person lies across them and is rocked gently from side to side.

Elaboration

Ask the group to find different ways for the person to get safely down from the 'back'. You will find that children are very imaginative; they invent slides, synchronized hoists, and many varied ways of extending this exercise.

> **Teaching point**
>
> This is an exercise of trust, both for the people being the 'back' as well as for the person lying on the back. The 'back' is also taking collective responsibility for the care of another.

Veronica Sherborne (1990) makes the point that human bodies are the best climbing apparatus. The human body has many possibilities for such use: to be climbed on or ridden on, for example, and these movements give continuous bodily feedback to the children thus engaged.

The following dramatized playtherapy scenes incorporate the movements described above, and also function as case history examples.

PLAYTHERAPY SCENES

The log story

Once upon a time, there was a very thick forest. There were so many trees that they were crowding each other out, and all their branches were tangled up together. (*Group stand very close together, intertwined.*) The forester decided that some of the trees would have to be cut down and taken down the river. (*Half the group become logs and the other half roll them down the hill.*) The logs are rolled down the hill and into the river where they float down to the farm. They float under bridges (*made by the group*), and at times they float so near each other that they get stuck. (*This guides proximity and distance of movement.*) When the logs come to the farm, they are pulled out of the water and left to dry on the bank.

The simple log story above (which is ecologically sound and non gender specific) shows the following movement and social progression:

(1) Whole group: body-mass – touching and intertwined
(2) Whole group to pairs: body-pairing – logs and log-pushers
(3) Pairs to individuals: body-individuation – floating down river
(4) Whole group: body-mass – at log jam

(5) Group to individual: body-individuation – log jam freed
(6) Individual to pair: body-pairing – log and log-pullers
(7) Pair to individual: body-individuation – logs drying

This story can be taken further with transformation – from logs to shelters, for example, depending upon the stage of the group.

The boat story

Once upon a time, some small boats were tied up in the harbour (*people in threes one behind the other*) resting; very gently rocking side-to-side. They decided to go out to sea to look for adventure. They all set off out of the harbour. (*Groups move themselves across the floor.*) The wind began to blow, the waves became stronger and the boats rocked from side to side. (*Groups sway, using larger movements.*) A big wave and gust of wind came up and blew the boats over and everyone was swimming in the sea. (*Boats disintegrate and individuals start to swim.*) All the people were huddled up in the sea, swimming around looking for their own boat. Gradually, the wind subsided and the waves got smaller and the people found their own boat. (*Small groups find each other.*) The boats decided that they had had a big adventure and went back to the harbour again. (*Boats in threes move across room.*) They arrived in the harbour, tied themselves up, and rested. (*People close eyes and lean and support each other.*)

This story takes people from relaxation to stimulation and back again – from the known to the unknown. It uses the following movement and social progression:

(1) Groups of three: touch and co-operation, bodies relaxed and still
(2) Bodies working together to move out to sea
(3) Bodies moving vigorously together
(4) Small group to individuals: bodies individuate, floating and swimming vigorously
(5) Individuals to small groups: bodies relating, re-discovering threes
(6) Small group relaxing and touching: bodies working together; return to harbour

It represents a maturational step when children can progress from working with a partner to working with a threesome. If children are not able to make this maturational step, the three will break up into a pair and an individual (less often, to three individuals).

Again, the basic story above can be built on using the different elements of weather; light and dark; visiting the world under the water.

Case history

I have used a variation of the above story with a remedial infant class with learning and behavioural difficulties. We progressed from the boat into the sea and then created the world of the sea with everyone choosing what they wanted to be. People chose to be pieces of coral, fish of different sorts and sizes, crabs, floating seaweed.

I then asked each child to describe their shape and colour and to show how they moved. (The children had been stimulated by a recent TV educational programme about the sea-bed.) After we had explored under the sea, we swam to the surface, found our boats, and sailed back to land again.

At this point, the class teacher peered through the door and asked if she could see what they were doing. The children returned to the sea-bed again, resumed their previous roles, and described their colours, shapes and movements. They were greeted by the following response: 'children, this is very silly. You saw that programme on a black-and-white television!' What does a hapless playtherapist do at this point?

On this particular occasion, I intervened and said, 'let me explain. We were *imagining* what colours were under the sea. I'm developing the use of language at the moment.' Honour seemed to be satisfied for the teacher and the children stopped looking crestfallen. (For further information, see Chapter 10 on working with staff.)

The magic forest story (Fig. 2.3)

Once upon a time, a group of small animals was travelling through the countryside. They came to a magic forest. (*Half the group act as forest as individual trees and half act as animals.*) The animals came into the forest looking for a resting place. (*Encourage the 'trees' to stand legs apart and body bent.*)

Each animal found a shelter and curled up inside. (*Tree creates a shelter with arms and legs on floor*) and the tree/shelter closed its doors and closed its windows. (*'Tree' body closes in to protect child.*)

During the night there were lots of noises in the forest (*noises made by trees*), but the creatures were quite safe. The next morning,

Fig. 2.3   The Magic Forest.

when the sun was up, the trees opened their doors and the small creatures stretched themselves and opened their eyes. They peered out of the window and decided to explore the forest. They came out of the shelter and decided to climb the tree (*'tree' acts as climbing frame for child to climb to hip or shoulders*) and looked out into the forest.

In the distance, the creatures could see some water and decided to go looking for food and drink. They climbed down from the tree and left their shelter and went off together.

The above story is much more advanced than the previous ones: everyone is in-role as tree/shelter or animal, although the emphasis is on movement. Movement is more detailed as opposed to the gross movement of the earlier stories; there is also more interaction. There is a range of responses required – tiredness, choices (which house?), trust (being looked after), support (solid climbing tree) and separation (leaving home again). The story also places more imaginative demands on the children. They are working first as two differentiated groups (although they remain individuals within the group) – tree-shelters and small animals – and then in pairs, contrasting from each group – one carer and one cared for – then differentiated into groups of individuals.

Elaborations

There are creatures in the forest and the small animals take one or all of the following courses of action:

- Go out to explore and then return to the safety of the tree/shelter
- Decide to live in the forest
- Find one magic creature in the forest who gives them a secret

Case history

I was asked to work with a mixed group of children with a mental handicap. Originally, I was expecting to work with six- to nine-year-olds, but when I arrived I was asked to take an integrated class which included ten- to thirteen-year-olds. (The older children were so large!) I decided to use the magic forest story and ask the older children to be the tree/shelters. I told the story as it is given above. The older children made very realistic forest sounds, yet were very protective of the small animals. I decided that there should be the sounds of a creature in the forest that might be good or might be bad and the small animals were going to discover what it was.

The children set off the 'next morning' and found a magic cat which had been trapped by a witch and they knew the magic word ('doughnuts') to set it free. The cat then joined their group and went off on the journey.

After we had finished, I was going to build another episode onto the story, but the older children said, 'It's our turn now. We want to be the little animals.' The younger children then became the trees and were literally 'stretched' as these lumbering lads and tall girls (all of them big for their age) curled up in their shelters.

The teacher later told me that this was the first time the older children had ever done anything where they might feel silly and that they had never done any dramatic play before.

SUMMARY

In this chapter we have looked at the normal stages of physical development from birth and considered various methods in body-play that can be re-experienced in therapy. We have defined the over-, under- and distortedly-held child and the balance needed between nurture and stimulation in order to effect repair.

NOTES

[1]   While supporting the increase of touch between parents and children and indeed between adults, I am also aware of the cultural restraints that modify our bodily behaviour. It is equally uneasy to have compulsory touch – which for many people feels like an invasion of body boundaries – than to have none at all.

REFERENCES

Cattanach, A. (1992) *Play Therapy with Abused Children*. London: Jessica Kingsley.

Garvey, C. (1977) *Play*. Glasgow: Fontana Books.

Gersie, A. (1986) 'Dramatherapy and Play'. In *Dramatherapy and Practice* 1. (Ed. S. Jennings). London: Routledge.

Jennings, S. (1986) *Creative Drama in Groupwork*. Bicester: Winslow Press.

Jennings, S. (1987) (Ed) *Dramatherapy Theory and Practice*. London: Routledge.

Jennings, S. (1992) (Ed) Dramatherapy Theory and Practice 2. London: Routledge.

Jennings, S. (in preparation) *Theatre, Ritual and Transformation*, London: Routledge.

Miller, A. (1981) *The Drama of Being a Child*. London: Virago.

Opie, I. and P. (1959) *The Lore and Language of Schoolchildren*. Oxford: Oxford University Press.

Sherborne, V. (1990) *Developmental Movement for Children*. Cambridge: Cambridge University Press.

Chapter 3

Projective Play

'For many children, and for most children
at certain times, some feature of their
environment presses too hardly upon them,
and the way out that is left to them is the
recreation in play of the same environment,
but with the painful features remodelled
to their heart's desire'.

Margaret Lowenfeld, 1935

In Chapter 2 we saw how the first year of a child's life is dominated by the child's experience of the human body and that toys, objects and other human beings (i.e. media) are experienced as extensions of that body. In this chapter we consider how the child develops the capacity to separate from media outside itself. The child is learning the boundaries of his or her own body and is able to experience various media as separate from, rather than as extensions of, the body. The media become less part of the child's body and more part of the child's world. This involves both separation and transformation as the child's body-self and internal world become part of an expanding external world. We could say that it is a transition of the child 'being the world' to the child being 'in the world'. As the child develops an expanding experience of being in the world, it develops resources to be able to describe it in non-verbal and verbal ways.

The transition from embodiment to projection is a gradual one, commencing towards the end of the first year and heightened by the child's urge to explore and its developing capacity to symbolize. As was seen in Chapter 1, the child's first symbol (what I term the dominant symbol) is usually the 'transitional object'.

STAGE 2: PROJECTION

Projection is stage 2 in the EPR developmental paradigm. Inevitably there is some overlap with stage 1 (Embodiment) as the child explores in a physical way the sensation of media outside its own body. Some materials assume particular importance and these include sand and water and finger paint; these will be discussed later in the chapter.

EARLY STAGES OF PROJECTION

Projective play, in which the child can create and re-create symbolic situations and worlds, is preceded by an extended time of exploratory play. Whereas in the embodiment stage the child explores its own body and immediate body world, this is now extended into sensory play through a variety of media and materials. Children will play with sand and water, finger-paint, Plasticine, food (and, when not supervised, sugar, washing-up liquid, feces, jelly, and so on). This is a time of discovery and sensory stimulation rather than one that involves making something. Too often adults will attempt to explain or impose their own interpretations on these explorations.

Gradually the child begins to exercise control over the media and begins to create patterns, shapes and groupings. Objects are fitted into space or separated according to shape or colour. Eye/hand co-ordination is practised, and manipulative dexterity develops through a variety of media play. Being able to balance something or create a pattern brings satisfaction in itself without necessarily having to lead to something else.

The early stages of projective play – the sensory stimulation of a variety of media; the play that is satisfying because of shape and balance; the play that solves a problem such as fitting one shape into another – are all part of the child's developing exploration and skill. It constitutes another step when such play becomes symbolic, i.e. when the groupings, shapes or patterns represent the child's world in a symbolic way. Such sensory and manipulative play develop both skills and imagination and will allow symbolic play to become increasingly rich.

A playtherapy vignette

A child came to the playgroup and said, 'I'm going to make a real mess today'. She proceeded to sink her hands and arms into the sand, pour water in, mix it up and let it ooze between her fingers. She then began to build a castle with a moat and bridge and placed shells and stones in the castle with a great degree of precision. It took a lot of patience to build the bridge as it kept falling away because the sand was damp. Eventually she was satisfied and said, 'Once upon a time there was a big mess, and the mess turned into a castle, and then, the castle became a mess again'. At this point she flattened the castle, stirred all the wet sand about and then pealed with laughter.

Teaching point

The above example illustrates exploratory, sensory and manipulative play, organized into a rhythm which the child finds satisfying. Compare this with the example of David in Chapter 4 where a very similar situation enables the possibility of therapeutic change.

DEVELOPED PROJECTIVE PLAY

As the child increasingly develops the capacity to pretend, we can observe an increase in symbolic play. Objects become toys: a brick, for example, can become a house or an animal; an animal can take on human characteristics. The child is projecting ideas and feelings into the media surrounding it. In projective play, the child is both creating and re-creating and formulating new constellations of past, present and future experience. Thus it is possible for the child to create an experience that is satisfying, to re-create a pleasurable or frightening experience, and to re-formulate the elements in new ways that demonstrate the possibility of change of outcome. This human capacity to project our experiences into media is harnessed in dramatherapy with adults into the technique known as 'sculpting'[1].

The stage of projection is a normal part of human development. Not all projective play is symbolic play; it can also be exploratory, sensory and manipulative. In therapeutic intervention, a child may need to learn or re-learn the capacity to play with and through media. It may need to achieve this before being able to symbolize its experience through projective play. Just as the child who has been deprived of bodily experience during the embodiment stage may need to re-experience and re-learn its 'body world', a child may also need to experience sensory, exploratory and manipulative play in order to be able to play projectively in symbolic form. Without this experience, children are likely to be impaired emotionally and cognitively and have difficulty making sense of their experience of the world. It is through the development of the imagination in symbolic play that the child processes its own experiences and creates new possibilities. The child who misses this stage of development, therefore – for whatever reason – is likely to be impaired.

DISRUPTION OR ABSENCE OF PROJECTIVE PLAY

Disruption of normal development

Children who have been hospitalized for severe illness or disability may well miss out on these important stages of play development, although it is encouraging to see that many hospitals place great store on the work of play teachers and nursery nurses. It may also be that families, or rather parents themselves, do not see the value of the play experiences, and will discourage play. They may see this as a short-cut to encourage a child to become an adult as quickly as possible; they may also place themselves in the role of teacher and direct their children's play. Others believe in encouraging the total freedom of the child and expect them 'to go and play', the sub-text of this being 'don't get in my way'.

Most Western cultures are very ambivalent about play and tend to use the word in a pejorative sense. Teachers and educationalists are therefore often hard-pressed to explain to parents the importance of play, both for its own sake, and as a precursor to other forms of learning.

Absence of projective play

Where there is a great emphasis on academic or professional achievement in a family, there can be a denial of the importance of play. This phenomenon is not confined to the professional classes: I have seen it as much with working-class families who wish something better for their children, as with professional and academic families. Often children of four and five years of age have enormous pressure put on them for academic achievement, with private tuition, educational videos and home-time programmed for formal learning. It is difficult for some parents to understand that the seeming time-wasting of 'play' will in itself develop a child's skills and intelligence.

Case history

Lena came to see me about her thirteen-year-old son whom she described as a delinquent. Lena came from Cyprus, had married a British soldier, and had two sons – Nikos, sixteen, and Johnnie, thirteen. She described her older son as successful and intelligent; her younger son on the other hand was a worry, kept her awake at nights, and would she thought come to a bad end. When I asked her to describe what Johnnie did, she burst into tears and said that she didn't know what to do. The main problem as she saw it was that he would not do his homework and always wanted to play football. 'I've gone out working to pay for extra classes', she said; 'I've tried so hard to be a good mother and provide him with things'.

Lena wanted both her sons to go to university and to have professions, perhaps as doctors or lawyers. She felt that she herself had been deprived of a good education and her husband, 'a good man', was only a soldier. This wasn't good enough for her boys and she was determined to provide them with better chances. Her husband did not figure much in these decisions, but supported her. He was away a lot but was always a dutiful husband and father.

Johnnie wasted his chances, she said, by wanting to play outside all the time, even pretending to have done his homework when he hadn't: 'He's lying to me – lying; so now I test him on everything when he says he's done it. Why should he lie to me? He will be a delinquent'.

It turned out that Johnnie had had private tuition from the age of six in reading and mathematics. Her struggle with him had been going on for several years to make him work. At school he was often referred to as 'a dreamer', and although he had not made brilliant academic progress, nevertheless he was not causing any concern; however, they had been disappointed that he had not been allowed to take a place in the sports team.

At this initial interview I suggested to Lena that she tried a compromise with her son in order to try and take the heat out of the situation. In the end we agreed that he could play football immediately after school, either at school or at home, and then would do his homework after he had had his supper. We also agreed that he would do only the homework set by the school and not any extra for the two weeks.

The school indicated that they could contain the situation without singling Johnnie out for individual therapy. They encouraged him in his sports and gave him feedback about the satisfactory standard of his academic work.

Lena came to see me again three weeks later, still a worried mother, but less 'on the boil'. I did not consider therapy to be necessary for her but she did need some help to understand normal adolescence and also to enable her to build a world for herself. She was able to tell me that she was very lonely in England and that her sole focus was her children. We had three sessions of talking together, looking at her own needs and at the importance of expanding her world. Johnnie continued to develop as a healthy teenager, infinitely more confident once he was both allowed and encouraged to play football.

Teaching point

In this example we may note how important it is to have an understanding of cultural norms and values. Contemporary Greek society places tremendous importance on early academic learning and achievement. This in Lena's case was exacerbated by her loneliness and isolation and at times by 'culture clash'[2].

DIRECTED PLAY

With some children, parents (and teachers too) feel that their play activity should be directed by the adult. The child is praised for reproducing what the adult wants. A child's endeavours will be paraded in front of other relatives, and experimentation is dismissed as 'silly' or 'nonsense'. The fundamental point that a child makes sense through nonsense is not understood[3]. Such children are allowed to play with construction sets and other toys which are seen as highly educational with a purpose; painting is by numbers and not allowed to be free; accuracy and reproduction through copying and tracing is praised and anything that might be a muddle, messy or dirty is discouraged. Toys are often miniature reproductions of adult objects: these include specific dressing-up clothes, toy dustpans and brushes, a designer Wendy-house and so on. Such parents become very daunted and even hurt when a child takes more pleasure in the box and wrapping in which the present arrived or when the child spends pocket-money on a box of old buttons at a jumble sale.

While it is true that one of the functions of play is to play out adult situations and roles and pastimes that children will encounter later in life, what is being missed is that the child's own imaginative and problem-solving resources are not being developed. Rigid play is likely to develop rigid people, and those children who have not developed their own resources are likely to have difficulties in dealing with new and unexpected situations. It is through our capacity to be creative that we learn to deal with life itself, as well as the obvious pleasure we can derive from creation in itself. The child who is unable to play projectively in symbolic form is deprived of the capacity to struggle with the world and to make sense of it. All it receives is the adult's view of the world through a very restricted telescope.

Projective play with no limits

In child development and family beliefs there is a school of thought that suggests the child should be allowed to develop with no intervention from adults: playing should be a completely free activity, and in this way the child will learn all it ever needs to learn. This approach is the antithesis of the above description of rigid play and can be equally stultifying to the child's growth. A child needs adults to be involved in play from time-to-time. From ten months old, the child will make the adult into an audience to watch performances. Children need adults to join in the struggle sometimes: to play *with* them, rather than to do it *for* them. Children also need adults to be able to set limits and boundaries to contain the play – the well-known 'tears before bedtime' situation.

A child who does not have an adult to play within some of the time will only play within its own experience or will create an experience with no boundaries, something that can be very frightening. Play needs to be both solitary, adult shared, and social – where others are true participants within the play – and not silent on-lookers or absent figures. Further examples of techniques for projective methods are described in Chapter 5.

PROJECTIVE METHODS

Projective play in therapy

I now want to concentrate on the use of projective play in symbolic play when it is being used for diagnostic, exploratory and reparative intervention. We shall see how this can be achieved through re-creation and new formulations of old structures where children are empowered to intervene in their life patterns. The methods described below form the basis of much dramatherapy work, particularly of what is known as 'sculpting' (see[1]), where clients of all ages make use of their capacity to project as a way of looking at their lives and life-decisions and at the possibility of new outcome.

The well-equipped playtherapy room includes a varied range of projective materials (see also Chapter 9) which may be used in directive and non-directive ways. These include animals of all sorts (domestic and wild), trees, gates, cars, aeroplanes, shells, stones, twigs, nesting dolls. The play must have some physical boundaries quite apart from the boundaries set by time and room-space and by the basic rules. Projective play may thus be carried out on a tray, a sandbox, a small table, a piece of sugar paper or a rug, for example. Not to provide these boundaries can create an experience that is very overwhelming for the child. Physical boundaries, however, act as a container for the experience. The child is invited to create a picture or to tell a story using the materials to hand. The child may do this spontaneously or may respond to an invitation. The child who is ready to tell their story will not need any coaxing or commanding – providing the atmosphere is safe and the materials are appropriate.

Case history

The following is a sculpt created by Trevor, a child who had been sexually abused.

He placed a heap of twigs and leaves in one corner of the tray: a rhinoceros, an elephant and a small dog in a row in descending order of size; lots of other toy animals in heaps and groups mixed together and not standing up; then some stones and trees at intervals.

TREVOR: 'It's the dog's story and the dog is unhappy because of the big animals. . . .'
THERAPIST: 'The rhinoceros and the elephant?'
TREVOR: 'Mmm, the 'oceros is big and scary and the elephant can't see but the dog can, and all the other animals can't see so the dog wants to hide and hides by the tree and the 'oceros says "I'm coming to get you" and the dog hates it and cries.'

At this point he starts to cry and changes to the first person and continues:

TREVOR: 'I hate him, hate him.'

He grabs the rhinoceros and flings it away. He has a heightened colour and looks momentarily relieved.

The temptation at a moment like this is to lead the child into disclosure work about details of the actual abuse. However, this is not a disclosure interview, and it is crucial to follow the child, if necessary with a prompt such as 'and what happens next in the story?' or 'what did the dog do then?' On this occasion the child continued without a prompt and said:

TREVOR: 'The dog had to keep finding new places to hide and not play the monster game, and the trees weren't big enough, so in the end (and he looked up with triumph and glee) the dog found the rubbish tip and the monster couldn't find him.'

He places the dog underneath the pile of leaves and twigs.

THERAPIST: 'So, in the rubbish tip, the dog felt quite safe?'
TREVOR: 'Nobody knows the tip because it's just a lot of rubbish, so nobody goes there, except the dog.' He looked at the picture for a few moments and then said 'That's the end of the story; goodbye.'
THERAPIST: 'So that's the end of the story and the dog feels quite safe in the rubbish tip.'
TREVOR: 'Yes; let's do something else now.'
THERAPIST: 'O.K., but let's put this story away first, and then you choose what you want to do next.'

Just as pictures and stories can be created, they must also be dismantled, and it is important that the children, where possible, do this for themselves. It is a means of transforming the play materials into their general functions again and diffusing the intensity with which they have been invested during the playtherapy.

Teaching point

Here, the materials are being 'de-roled', as in a piece of drama-work, and the process should not be hurried. It is not a question of tidying them away, but of allowing them to become neutral again, ready for any future work.

   After this story and the de-roling, Trevor wanted to play very boister-
ously in the soft corner with cushions and soft toys:

TREVOR: 'I'm going to bury you.'

He proceeds to pile the cushions and toys on top of me.

TREVOR: 'You can breathe, can't you?'

The answer he seemed to anticipate was 'yes', and in any case I could
breathe perfectly well.

THERAPIST: 'Yes, I can breathe.'

He piles more cushions.

TREVOR: 'Can you now?'

I was beginning to get very uncomfortable and was pretty sure that he was
using me to test something for himself. I push my head out and say:

THERAPIST: 'It's getting difficult to breathe.'
TREVOR: 'You do that to me now.'

I pile a few things, and ask:

THERAPIST: 'Can you breathe now?'
TREVOR: ''Course I can, put lots more on!'

I add a few cushions:

THERAPIST: 'Can you breathe now?'
TREVOR: 'Yes, put lots more! . . . .'

I add some more cushions and toys:

THERAPIST: 'That's it; I'm not putting any more there. No, that's enough;
we'll stop while you can still breathe.'

There is a pause, and then:

TREVOR: 'Alright then. You be the monster and make no noise.'

I think he has said 'and make a noise', so I reply:

THERAPIST: 'What sort of noise?'
TREVOR: 'NO noise. You are a silent monster.'

I crouch outside the cushions and say very quietly:

THERAPIST: 'I am a silent monster and I don't make any noise. The creature in the cushions can't hear me because I don't make any noise!'

Gradually there is movement in the pile of cushions and Trevor slowly emerges, obviously not wanting to be seen by the monster, so I do not look at him. He holds up a cushion and brings it down on my back, and says:

TREVOR: 'The monster is dead. Go on, make a dying noise.'

I provide some suitable moans and groans and then 'expire'. He goes a few paces away and takes a flying leap, landing on the cushions:

TREVOR: 'You see; the monster is dead, he can't even make dead noises now, or quiet ones.'
THERAPIST: 'It's soon time to stop now, so I am going to be me again and not the monster.'

As I sit up, he looks very satisfied and says:

TREVOR: 'Good story, isn't it? I want to do it again next time.'

The above stories could be interpreted in many different ways, depending on the reader's particular orientation (see Chapter 1). Perhaps a useful exercise would be to try analysing the story from Freudian, Jungian, Kleinian and Piagetian viewpoints; however, try to consider also what it meant for the child in the here and now?

Let us look at the two stories, both as it turned out using different projective techniques, in terms of what the child wanted to do.

In the sculpt, he created a representation of how the abusive situation felt: the rhinoceros father, elephant mother and dog-child being the main protagonists. The heaps of other animals were other adults who 'never see'; trees and stones were not big enough to hide in, and the rubbish tip is the safe place.

It is crucial at this point that the therapist not only *sees* what the child needs to be seen but also hears what the child wants to be heard. The picture enabled me to see his own view of his situation. There are many themes, the dominant themes being:

- People not seeing (others in the child's environment)
- 'Monster games' from which he could not escape
- A place of safety, in this case the rubbish tip

In fact, the child had spelled out his needs more clearly than could be done in any case conference, through his projective play.

Within the play he is already attempting to change the outcome of the monster game that he cannot escape. He is able to fling the rhinoceros away and thereby take control. It is important to pace oneself with the child. For example, a therapist might have been tempted to pursue the above picture and look at the people who had not seen and the people who (presumably) now did see. What was the role of the mother in all this? How might the elephant be developed in the picture? This might be appropriate for future work, but at this time the child was self-directing and made it clear when he wanted to end the story. My own intervention was purely to allow the ending, i.e. with the de-roling of the toys, so that they could become neutral again.

The same child himself directed the next story, and this time wanted me to be a part of it. I was to be the 'no-noise monster' that he was able to destroy. Again, it was important for him to feel in control and change the outcome himself. In the first part of the story, when he asked me to be buried in the cushions, again it would have been easy to interpret rather than to deal with his actual needs (the cushions, for example, could represent the womb and the emergence – the birth experience – but that did not seem to be an explanation that furthered what the child was actually engaged with). He continued piling cushions onto me until I imposed a limit and he was then able to demonstrate that he could tolerate even more cushions than I could. In fact, he wanted me to pile on yet more, but again I set a limit. It was not clear at this time how much the cushions represented the actual abuse with an adult's weight crushed on top of him and him not being able to breathe and fearful of dying. What was obvious was that the cushions could become the safe place, like the rubbish tip, from which he could emerge to kill the silent monster.

In reflection afterwards I thought that perhaps silent monsters were more scary than noisy ones; especially those that appeared to play ordinary 'I'm coming to get you' games which turned out to be far more sinister.

> *Teaching point*
>
> As the child's world expands, so do the means whereby, and through which, the child can play. Already in the above case history example we can see how the second story began to involve the therapist 'in-role'.

PROJECTIVE MEDIA

Earlier in this chapter and also in Chapter 9 (*Playtherapy Resources*), I list a range of projective materials for use in playtherapy. However modest the budget, the important thing is to have some contrast and choices between, for example, messy and non-messy play (finger paints and felt pens), between concrete and symbolic toys (family dolls and animal families).

Sensory projective play

Play with sand and water and finger paint acts as one of the bridges between the embodiment and projection stages, and children who are deprived of sensory experiences need plenty of time to experiment and explore. This can be a time of sheer wonder and magic.

Water play

Use washing up bowls with contrasting temperatures of water to develop sensory awareness through the child splashing, feeling, trickling and all the other experiences associated with 'water words'; elaborate the play with bubbles as well as containers, funnels and so on.

> *Teaching point*
>
> This is a clear example where the 'educational' and the 'therapeutic' overlap and in my view it is entirely relevant to enable the playtherapist to encourage sensory 'repair' play. It is also worth noting that children with 'bed-wetting' problems have, through this play, been able to control their physical body through being able to control water *outside of themselves*.

Sand and water play

Ideally, have a tray of wet and a tray of dry sand – larger washing up bowls can be used but are rather deep; alternatively, cat litter trays can be used since they are about the right size if rather shallow. The wet and dry sand can be experienced for its own sake – some sand can be controlled and some not. Sand can also be used to build landscapes, buildings and other structures.

Teaching point

It is very important for the child to play with 'natural sub-stances' such as sand and water to which may be added stones, shells, twigs, leaves, grasses and so on. Such play allows primary sensation.

Creating or sculpting the story or scene

The most detailed method here is the Lowenfeld 'World Technique' (see Chapter 2) where the child chooses from a vast array of toys and objects. However, the child may also be enabled to tell the projective story with modest numbers of small toys, objects (including natural ones) and a wet sand tray.

Teaching point

As has been emphasized throughout this book, playtherapists must be careful not to impose their own view of the child's story. The sculpted picture in the sandtray may be the first time that the child has been able to articulate its own life crisis and what is needed is the therapist's attention. A child will so easily share its story in this way that we must beware of being 'predators', especially as we find some images 'interesting'.

Finger paint play

An A4 piece of paper is usually large enough for finger painting. There should be a choice of paint colours. Children who have been kept obsessively clean will often avoid something so messy. However, there is usually a progression from using one finger to using both hands. The child will create shapes and patterns and sometimes incorporate toys and other media into the picture.

Teaching point

The use of finger paint, because it cannot be controlled, gives a very direct expression of the inner world which may well be 'a mess' or a 'black splodge' or 'a pooey picture'.

The extract below comes from a chapter entitled 'Art therapy as part of the world of dyslexic children'. The author presents us with a very clear therapeutic setting where there are choices of material, themes and outcome. There is an echo from the Lowenfeld quotation at the beginning of this chapter where the child also needs to repair the damage – i.e. to create the perfect or romantic vision, the 'heart's desire' as well as the more painful reality of the traumatic happening[4].

'We had on offer a range of art materials – clay, paper, paints, scissors, crayons. They could choose their materials and subject matter. I would suggest a theme but this was optional. I was impressed with the intensity and absorption encouraged by the creative process. Sometimes the desired communication was quickly achieved, and its creator wished for some confidential time to share this process. The group was seldom so competitive as to prevent this. Often the individual shared long-buried secrets or faced up to previously inadmissable realities. As the children were away from home, there was a tendency to romanticise their families and their relationship with them. Although very painful, they often revealed the opposite scenario, a more authentic picture of their relationship with their families.'

Tish Feilden, 1990

Story play

The early story

Children, as we can see, will share their 'world' or story and often, this will be their experience of the damaging situation which may be in the past or continuing in the present. It is also important for the child to be able to express this story in time – 'has this picture always been like this?' 'was the picture different a long time ago? or before you moved house?' and so on. For many children the 'early story' may have positive memories and this story may help to bring about hope in an otherwise despairing situation.

The journey story

The 'early story' where it is different may well lead the child, with the help of the therapist, into the 'journey story' where the child is able to tell the story through pictures, sand, objects, toys, dolls' house, and so on[5]. The child can thus experience the moves from one state of being to another. This can assist the child not only to 'make sense' of the story but also give a feeling of 'movement' – i.e. that things can move on and change.

Further playtherapy methods are described in Chapter 5 where there is a detailed description of many projective methods including 'container play' with the use of special boxes that contain objects and scenes as well as boxes that the child can actually climb inside.

SUMMARY

In this chapter we have looked at the function of projective play in the normal development of the child and what happens to the child's growth if this does not take place. This included:

- Absence of projective play
- Rigid projective play
- Uncontained projective play

We next considered how projective play could be used in therapeutic intervention, differentiating between play that is exploratory and sensory, manipulative and problem-solving, and that which is symbolic in terms of creating and re-creating the child's experience. The next chapter looks at the third developmental stage – that of role, and how it integrates into the developmental paradigm.

NOTES

[1] The dramatherapy and playtherapy technique known as sculpting is described in detail in *Dramatherapy with Families, Groups and Individuals* (Jennings, 1990). It provides a means of representing a scene, situation or event in the past present or future through static objects (small objects such as toys or bigger ones such as chairs or people themselves – sometimes referred to as body sculpts). Thus the therapist might suggest that the client(s) create a sculpt called 'my life now' or 'my family now' or 'the old house' or 'how I would like my life to be'. This technique is paradoxical because on the one hand it concretizes the experience and creates a structure for it, but on the other it usually moves into symbolic shifts of perception and the possibility of movement in the status quo.

[2] There is not scope in this book to elaborate in any depth on the anthropological data that exist concerning the cultural dimensions of play. However, the subject should not be allowed to pass without pointing the reader to the delightful chapter entitled 'Deep play: a description of the Balinese cockfight' by Geertz in Bruner (below).

[3] Shakespeare well understood the importance of 'nonsense', perhaps best described by the character of Bottom in *A Midsummer Night's Dream*:

> 'I see a voice; now will I to the chink,
> To spy and I can hear my Thisbe's face.'

> 'Sweet Moon, I thank thee for thy sunny beams;
> I thank thee, Moon, for shining now so bright;
> For by thy gracious, golden, glittering gleams,
> I trust to take of truest Thisbe sight.'

See also Chukovsky (1963) 'The sense of nonsense verse' and Weir (1962) 'Playing with language' in Bruner (below).

[4] We can see that play is multi-media and in the Playtherapy Method, I include all forms of play in the developmental paradigm. However, we should not ignore the fact that arts therapists specialize in particular art forms and there is excellent work being done by art therapists who work with children, as well as by music therapists, dramatherapists and dance-movement therapists. I am reminded of my colleague Cathy Ward, working in a Family Centre, who has integrated systemic family therapy and art therapy thus being able to explore the several worlds and their shapes and patterns.

[5] Many playtherapists pay great attention to play with dolls' houses – I do use them but find they have certain limitations. They cannot be manipulated and some children find they cannot manage the very

small furniture. I have used a 'good' house that I stress is not to be broken and another house that I allow to be bashed around. However, I find that many children create the house in painting and in the sand and various object play.

REFERENCES

Bruner, J.S., Jolly, A. & Sylva, K. (Eds) (1976) *Play, Its Role in Development*, Harmondsworth: Penguin.

Cattanach, A. (1992) *Play Therapy with Abused Children*, pp 56–67. London: Jessica Kingsley.

Chukovsky, K. (1963) 'The Sense of Nonsense Verse'. In Bruner, *op cit*.

Feilden, T. (1990) 'Art Therapy as part of the World of Dyslexic Children'. In *Art Therapy in Practice* (Ed. by M. Liebmann). London: Jessica Kingsley.

Geertz, C. (1976) 'Deep Play: a Description of the Balinese Cockfight'. In *Play. Its Role in Evolution and Development* (Ed. by J.S. Bruner, A. Jolly & K. Sylva), pp 656–74. Harmondsworth: Penguin.

Jennings, S. (1990) *Dramatherapy with Families, Groups and Individuals*. London: Jessica Kingsley.

Kalff, D. (1980) *Sandplay*, pp 23–39. Santa Monica, Ca: Sigo Press.

Liebmann, M. (Ed) (1990) *Art Therapy in Practice*. London: Jessica Kingsley.

Lowenfeld, M. (1935; 1992 repr) *Play in Childhood*. London: MacKeith Press.

Oaklander, V. (1978) *Windows to our Children*. Moab, Utah: Real People Press.

Weir, R. (1962) 'Playing with Language' In Bruner, *op cit*.

Chapter 4

Role and Dramatic Play

'Eddie sits on the mattress, picks up the bottle.

EDDIE: Drink, now?

MARY: 'lright.

Mary starts to drink.

EDDIE: Nice?

MARY: 'Mm'.

Mary drinks. Then Eddie turns his head slightly to look at Brenda, to acknowledge his pleasure that Mary is drinking. This small gesture causes Mary to feel very bad, and she spits the milk out, in Eddie's face.

MARY: Wrong. WRONG. Eddie!

Eddie himself takes a drink of the bottle, and spits it over Mary. Mary looks astonished. Then Eddie gives the bottle to Mary, who drinks and spits over Eddie. She begins to chuckle. Eddie drinks and spits. Mary drinks and spits. Laughs. Eddie takes the bottle, drinks and swallows.

EDDIE: Glug-ug-ug. Glug-ug-ug-ug.

Mary laughs, she takes the bottle, drinks.

MARY: *Glug-ug-ug-ug.*'

from *Mary Barnes*: a Play by David Edgar

STAGE 3: ROLE

In Chapters 2 and 3 we considered the first two broad stages of the developmental paradigm – embodiment and projection. This chapter is concerned with stage 3 of the developmental paradigm, that of role. Although the word role orginated in the theatre from the roll of paper on which an actor's part was written, it has come to mean the different sorts of behaviours that people learn in order to be fully socialized adults. It is a term frequently used by clinicians who will often claim that role has nothing to do with drama. I use the word 'character' as well as role in order to high-light a more fulsome sense of human beings and their many facets.

The above quotation from David Edgar is a superb example of therapist and patient engaging through a dramatized situation. On closer examination we can see that it involves a sensory experience (embodiment) as well as playing a role. Notice how, the therapist takes on a role – not as a 'mother' to Mary's 'child' but as another 'child', and through becoming a child too, is able to role model some less frightening behaviours for Mary.

From the age of a few months, a child is already exploring in proto-play the imitation of sounds and expressions it receives from the restricted world around it. The child attempts to reproduce sounds, those made by its mother or close carer and other sounds in the environment. By six months the child is able to imitate both movements and sounds and react to surprises. By twelve months imitation has progressed to the capacity *to pretend to be* the mother and also the creation *of an audience*.

THE ROLE OF THE 'TRANSITIONAL OBJECT'

In Chapter 3 the significance of sand and water media as bridges between the embodiment and projection stages was discussed. I want to include in this chapter more discussion on the 'transitional object' – the first loved object or toy – and its relationship with play development. Although the 'transitional object' exists as a toy or piece of cloth outside the child and is therefore a projected symbol – nevertheless it integrates all three stages in the following ways:

- It has a physical dimension – the child strokes, caresses, hugs, smells the object (embodiment)
- It is a projective symbol – the child invests it with a multiplicity of meanings (projection)
- It takes on roles – it becomes different characters, is named and accompanies the child in its adventures

Although in Winnicottian terms it represents the breast/mother, we can observe that it also takes on several aspects of role. It personifies these roles and becomes a dramatic character within the child's dialogue and actions. It is usually named; the child talks to it; the child asks it questions, and then answers on its behalf. In other words, the child has begun to take the role of the other or to 'role-reverse' using psychodramatic language.

Teaching point

It is important to note that dramatic play develops by itself – that is, adults do not have to teach a child to role reverse, it happens spontaneously. However, many adults assume that role reversal is a very difficult technique that many people cannot do. *We need to continually question how it was that we became cut off from our dramatic roots and have had to re-learn things that we always knew!*

During projective play through media, the child is able to take on the voice and gestures of others and to expand its range of role-playing. We may say that the child is now able to personify others; to take their roles in play. To be able to do this, the child has begun to identify with 'another'. Through being able to identify with 'other', the child is beginning to develop its own identity. Just as earlier the necessity of the emergence of the child's body-self before it was able to acquire a body-image was described, it is important to realize here that the child can only develop an identity by being able to identify with others. This process is described as role-taking. Thus, by two years of age, the dramatic persona of the child has developed as follows:

imitation → pretending to be → personifying

During this time, most of the role-playing is enacted through projective materials – toys and animals, puppets and dolls. By four to five years old, the child takes on more and more roles for itself, rather than projecting roles through media outside itself. The role-playing has become more complex and includes dressing-up and creating environments within which to play roles. Scenes and stories are enacted, with and without audiences, and other people are included in the dramatic play. The play-world of the child has become more and more dramatized in form and content, and outcome is important. Vocal and physical range is expanded and dramas consist of both everyday situations and imagined events. From five years, the child is able to improvise scenes and characters and to take on social roles and fantasy roles. Usually at around seven years we refer to the child's ability to engage in drama that has grown out of dramatic play. The following is a developmental progression of the child's emergent role-skill:

(1) *Proto-play* – imitation of sounds, gestures; reactions (copied)
(2) *Pretend* – to be mother, the dog, the monster (learned through imitation)
(3) *Personify* – mother, family members, TV character (variation, not just replication); beginning of identification and role-taking
(4) *Projective roles* – through objects and toys; role-taking
(5) *Enactment* – of roles/scenes; using environment; begins to include others
(6) *Dramatic play* – separation out of enactment from other play activities; dressing-up; stories; family and social scenes
(7) *Drama* – all of the above, and the ability to improvise, test ideas and repeat them; refine performance; practice drama skills; role-flexibility.

WHY IS THE CAPACITY TO ROLE-PLAY SO IMPORTANT?

We can say that we enact the drama of our lives through a series of tried and tested roles. The basis of these has been laid out in early play experience and refined through childhood and adolescence. To achieve this, we not only need the time and space to play, but also a range of role-models in our family and social environment with whom we can identify. It is through our roles that we are able to construe ourselves and the world in which we live in a balanced and flexible way. It is through our roles that we are able to manage our lives satisfactorily and also to deal with the unexpected. Our capacity to role-play helps us to understand ourselves and others, that is by playing a role, we not only learn about another, we also learn more about ourselves. Therefore, we can say that role-playing mediates between ourselves and others and is the means whereby we develop both an individual and a social identity. The disadvantaged outcome for adults who have not been allowed this process within their normal development is yet another question. Let us look here at what happens in a child's development when the process of role-exploration and development has not taken place or is too rigidly imposed or is inappropriate.

In Chapter 2 we looked at the effect on the child when it is under-held, over-held and distortedly-held. In Chapter 3 we considered the child who is not allowed to play projectively, who is directed to play, and who has no limits or no participating adult. We can now consider absence of role-model, rigid role-model and distorted role-models and their effect in the rearing process.

ABSENCE OF ROLE-MODELS

The child who has been subject to a variety of environments and carers or who has been hospitalized from an early age or placed in an institution, is usually without significant role-models. This means that the child does not have a consistent role-model(s) with whom to identify in order to develop a sense of self, that is the beginnings of identity. As we know from the writings on wolf children (Gleitman, 1986), a child takes on the body actions and skills of those closest to it [1]. The child with minimal role-models is abandoned to a confusing world of impressions with no core identity. All the impressions an infant normally receives from the first few weeks – in the way it is cared for, talked to and played with – are absent. It is not surprising that some children have been considered organically damaged as a result of such emotional and social deprivation.

It is important as the child develops that others – and not only the primary carer – inhabit the child's world in order for a greater range of role-models to be available. The child is thus able to develop more flexibility. Many children have a paucity of real life role-models and an increasing number of media models. The media model only provides a fictive model – not in itself negative – but this becomes negative if it is at the expense of live models.

Some children have the resources to survive enormous deprivation. Other children become seriously impaired in all areas of their development – physical, emotional, mental and indeed spiritual. Many will survive with but a single role with which to cope with living. This role may indeed become psychotic as the child is unable to deal with the demands of everyday reality.

Case history

A five-year-old girl was admitted to a large hospital for children with severe organic damage. She had been removed from the parents' home when it was discovered that she had been left alone, tied to a cot and intermittently fed with a bottle and rusks. The parents had said that she could not do anything, and they had to care for her all the time; that there was something wrong with her. The child was unable to walk or sit without support and had no language or responses to mild stimuli.

In the hospital it was assumed that she would need to be cared for and would remain totally dependent for basic physical needs. However, the care staff began to realize, even with the limited amount of time spent with her, that she was beginning to respond. For example, she took obvious pleasure in being bathed and dried with a towel and tried to splash the water. One of the nurses used to talk to her all the time she was looking after her: 'now, over her head, that's right; and one, two, three buttons . . . see if the water is right . . . yes – and into the water . . . let's wash her tummy . . . tickle, tickle . . .' and so on. The child started to try and shape some of the sounds and echo the nurse . . .' (th)ere (w)e (g)o . . .'. The staff suggested that she was merely imitating and might learn some basic skills through copying but would not be able to progress to independent action or thought.

This particular nurse persisted and enlisted the assistance of the nursery teacher, who used very basic play techniques – singing games, action songs and so on. The child developed very quickly: she was already sitting up unaided and was observed to pull herself up to standing. Her language-learning was very slow and she relied heavily on pointing and making noises to get what she wanted. However, she was now able to be tested and it was suggested that, although there was some retardation, it was impossible to say how much could be organic and how much environmental.

The nursery arranged special classes for her and the learning was reinforced by the nursing staff to the extent that within eighteen months she had already progressed to the learning stage of a three to four-year-old. The encouraging outcome was that she was eventually fostered in a new home and was able to attend an ordinary primary school.

Teaching point

What is important for our understanding of role-modelling is that it seems that this particular child's home did not provide any care or interaction with either a significant other or others. The child had been left alone apart from minimal attention to basic needs and had not developed either physically or in terms of language or socially. Her initial admission to hospital meant that she obtained some primary care similar to that of a baby: from this the normal developmental stages began to emerge, starting with embodiment and imitation. If she had been merely left in the hospital without the type of intensive care from the particular nurse who talked and played, it is likely that she would not have developed very far.

RIGID ROLE-MODELS

Many children are born into a family environment where there is a high degree of expectation on the child before it is even born. All parents, to a certain extent, have the notion of creating a 'dream baby' who will live up to their fantasies of the perfect child. Most parents relax their dream baby ambitions as the reality of a child becomes more and more part of their lives. However, some parents seek to mould a child by imposing a set of values and behaviours (as we saw with prescribed play) which start from birth with educational stimulus and rigid regimes.

As stated earlier, very often play activity is restricted to that which can be perceived as 'useful' and 'clean', and role-behaviour is an attempt to reproduce adult behaviour – norms and manners that are considered acceptable. Appropriate life and social skills are modelled and taught by rote and example. The parents themselves usually have a rigid role-relationship with prescribed limits as to what is appropriate for men and women and such behaviour conditions both the individual and also 'people like us'. The child responds by desperately wanting to conform in order to get praise from its parents. This in turn rarely happens as its efforts are rarely good enough. Often the child ends up dispirited and depressed and may be further confused if he or she is witness to other adult behaviour that does not fall within the categories that have been prescribed for the child.

Role-model vignettes

The following exchange was overheard in the toy department of a large store:

MOTHER: 'What do you want to spend your birthday money on?'
CHILD: 'Some soldiers.'
MOTHER: (with a sigh) 'All right, let's look at some nice soldiers.'
CHILD: 'I want some soldiers with a tank.'
MOTHER: 'No you don't, dear, you'd like some of these nice red and grey ones' (showing the child some crusaders).
CHILD: 'I don't want those ones – I want these' (pointing to some army soldiers). 'These have got guns.'
MOTHER: 'No, you don't want ones with guns. Let's have these. . . .'

A colleague had made a party for a group of four-year-olds for her son's birthday. Their going-home present was some liquorice allsorts that she had wired with striped wrapping paper and a lace doily into a bunch of flowers. One of the boys' fathers when he came to fetch his son, hissed in the child's ear:

FATHER: 'Don't stand like that, you look like a bridesmaid!'

The following was overheard in an infant class where one five-year-old boy was talking to another:

1ST CHILD: 'They always say you mustn't raise your voice 'cos it's not nice; but Daddy's always shouting at Mummy.'
2ND CHILD: 'Does he hit her as well?'

Case history

David had been assessed and admitted for playtherapy after there had been complaints from the school about his disruptive behaviour. One teacher had already left and another was on sick leave, and the Head said that David had been the cause. The report said that he systematically undermined the teacher in her role. He constantly challenged everything she said, refused to co-operate unless she explained why he had to do something, and was very obsessive about his clothes and possessions. Other children rejected him and he was very aggressive in sports.

In the first playtherapy session, he came into the room and looked around him. The playtherapist greeted him and told David her name and was about to tell him about the playroom; however, he pre-empted her:

DAVID: 'Why am I here?'
THERAPIST: 'This is a playroom where people learn how to play. I understand from your teachers that you find playing difficult.'
DAVID: 'Playing is silly and a waste of time.'
THERAPIST: 'Well, we have a whole hour to waste. Have a look round the room and see if there is anything you would like to play with.'
DAVID: 'It's silly. . . .'
THERAPIST: 'Maybe there are some things in the room that aren't. I agree that some of the things are silly.'

David wandered around the room, glancing at the equipment and toys and kicked a soft ball in a desultory way, and then turned back to the therapist.

DAVID: 'Do you like working here . . . playing?'
THERAPIST: 'Yes, I enjoy working with children through play, and there are always some surprises.'

Teaching point

This intervention by a trainee playtherapist was, I thought, quite brilliant in that she did not get into the fight. Rather than defending play, she agreed that it was a waste of time [2]. Her role-modelling which modified his statement that 'all' playing is silly to 'some' playing is silly, both affirmed the child, but allowed some scope for movement in attitude.

DAVID: (looking straight at her) 'What do you mean, surprises?'
THERAPIST: 'There are all sorts of people and all sorts of play here, and not everyone plays in the same way – so I have surprises.'
DAVID: 'You don't mind then: you don't get angry if someone plays in a . . . in a . . . mess?'
THERAPIST: 'No, I don't get angry at mess. Some play is more messy than other sorts of play, and some play is very messy.'
DAVID: 'If I tell you what to do, will you do it?'
THERAPIST: 'You mean, will I make a mess if you ask me to?'
DAVID: 'Yes – will you?'
THERAPIST: 'All right. You can tell me something messy to do, then I can tell you something messy to do.'
DAVID: (hovering) 'No; you do it first, and then I'll decide. You might give me something that gets me very messy.'
THERAPIST: 'Let's make a bargain: you won't tell me something to play that is very messy and then I won't tell you something that is very messy.'

Teaching point

Notice how the therapist has enabled David to express himself within his own frame of reference without loss of face. He has checked out whether or not she gets angry and whether she will do something on his behalf. Implicit in this instruction is that he is asking her to role-model a new piece of behaviour. She agrees, but keeps it within a therapeutic negotiation: he has a responsibility as well. His concern is that she will ask him to do something so extreme that his clothes will become marked. Probably this anxiety is also that he will lose control and really create a mess. However, within the play she is able to contain the anxiety and agree something that is acceptable and not too threatening.

DAVID: 'Alright. I want you to – pour the water in the sand and make a puddle. . . .'

The therapist does exactly that and talks as though to herself:

THERAPIST: 'I'm pouring the water into the sand and making it all slippy sloppy in a puddle. (David looks on with apprehension.) I want you to – take a spade and put the wet sand in the red bucket.'
DAVID: 'That's not hard – that's easy.' (He scoops the sand into the bucket and smooths down the top. He then turns to the therapist.) 'Can I turn it over like a sand-castle?'

Before she can reply, he has turned the red bucket over and lifted it up with his hands. All the wet sand goes into a heap because it is so wet. Some of the wet sand is on his hands and he looks fearful. He looks at the therapist uncertainly:

DAVID: 'What shall I do now?'
THERAPIST: 'We can try and make the sand-castle again, or you can wash your hands and we'll do something else – or we can do the game again of telling each other things to play.'

David went to the sink and immediately washed his hands and then returned to the therapist and asked her to make the sand-castle. She said that they could do it together and she showed him how they could put more dry sand in so that the castle wasn't so sloppy.

This play-intervention continued over an initial three months, through which David learned how to play, and play with mess. At each session he was preoccupied with the word 'mess' and wanted to create more and more. The therapist was careful to keep it within limits so that each experience was contained and did not get out of control.

Teaching point

Some people may have felt that David should have been encouraged to create as much mess as possible; however, I think the therapist was very wise in her gradual intervention. David so clearly needed to test his own boundaries, checking that he would not be overwhelmed. This demonstrates yet again how most children are self regulators.

The other important point here is that David is returning to a household which does not allow mess. Skilled intervention with the parents eventually brought about the idea of David having a playroom where he was allowed to make some mess.

He was still a very lonely child and now that his behaviour had modified at school, teachers suggested that he stayed to attend the various groups and clubs after school hours. His parents eventually agreed and there was a turning point when his dad came to watch him play in a Saturday match. It seemed that an integration between home and school, parental expectations and his own achievements, might just be possible.

DISTORTED ROLE-MODELS

Some readers may feel that the above example was a very distorted piece of role-modelling. However, I want to differentiate between the type of role-model that is an exaggerated piece of normal behaviour, i.e. where the existing behaviours can be modified, and the type of distortion that can occur when there has to be a fundamental change in the model and a major resolution of the child's experience. For example, in the above vignette, when David's parents modified their attitude and felt very affirmed as parents when they provided him with a playroom, David himself became more flexible. With the other role-models he acquired in school, therapy, and after-school activities, he was also able to identify with a range of behaviour which in turn made his own roles less stereotyped.

I consider a distorted role-model to be any behaviour that the child *witnesses* that is inappropriate to both the relationship and age, and any behaviour *towards* the child that is inappropriate to relationship and age. Most of such behaviours are punishable by law, although some categories of cruelty are not always easy to identify and prove. Within this range must come both physical and sexual abuse of the child and also of others in the family. Other possibilities are being a witness or an accomplice to other criminal acts such as fraud, burglary, and so on.

As both witness and/or victim or accomplice, a child is being subjected to a situation which he or she is unable to understand. This produces a distortion both of the way such children perceive the world and in the way they experience themselves. We have already stated that the child develops an identity through the processes of both identification and introjection of the role-model and we can see how the distorted role-model leads to a chaotic experience of self and other. Since as human beings we try to resolve chaos and uncertainty, the resultant behaviour usually finds a way of accommodating the distortion.

It is well known that many victims of child sexual abuse grow up to be perpetrators themselves or else become repeated victims in every sexual encounter. Others develop anorexia nervosa in an attempt to bring physical control into a situation where there has been a loss of normal control. Victims of violence often become violent in turn or else continue to find themselves as the receivers of violence. A child who is witness to violent language as the only means of communication may well choose not to speak at all.

Judicious playtherapy intervention may provide the opportunity for the child to re-experience a less distorted sense of self and other, and to allow re-modelling to take place.

Case history

Sarah was referred for playtherapy as a fourteen-year-old girl suffering from anorexia nervosa. She was a popular girl at school and especially enjoyed all sports and gymnastics. She put a lot of energy and time into these. She trained daily, jogging first thing in the morning and working out in the gym after school. She had received a lot of affirmation for her sports activities and her mother had said in an interview that she thought sports were good for girls as it kept them fit and out of mischief.

It wasn't until she collapsed at a training session that her GP became involved and discovered that Sarah weighed five stone (her height was 5 ft 7 in). It transpired that she had been able to avoid most family meals owing to the preoccupations with sport and had used her dinner money to purchase low-calorie meals. Her parents had been very shocked that their daughter was diagnosed as ill and in need of both physical and psychological treatment.

At her first session, she came in with a beaming smile and asked what I wanted her to do, saying, 'I've never done anything like this before, so you will have to tell me what you want.'

I felt how much easier it would be to fall into her presented role of well-being, smiling and friendly, and to take on the role of telling her what to do with her ingenuous innocence. I explained that I had seen the medical reports; that there were concerns about her weight and health, and that it was my job as playtherapist to see if there were any useful areas we could explore together.

SARAH: 'But I'm fine now. I'd just overdone the training a bit and forgotten to eat regularly because I was so busy. I have a very full timetable with sports and school work – but I'm OK.'

> **Teaching point**
>
> When someone is established as an anorectic it is quite un-
> helpful to get into a debate about eating habits and exercise
> unless the person knows that change is crucial and has the
> necessary motivation. Generally anorectic people are quite
> capable of maintaining the role they wish to present and
> will go to great lengths to avoid detection of destructive be-
> haviour. It can be helpful to see anorexia as a distorted role
> and to consider the possible role-modelling that has brought
> it about.

THERAPIST: 'I am not challenging you when you say you feel fine. You already know the concern of the doctor and your parents. However, what does interest me is that you feel fine and they think otherwise. Why do you think there's a difference?'

SARAH: 'Everyone is just making a fuss really, just because I overdid it. Mummy and Daddy weren't at all worried. They're terribly pleased at what I'm doing – the sports and so on. They've only become nervy because of what the doctor said, and then the doctor at the hospital.'

THERAPIST: 'So, before you collapsed, neither of your parents were worried about you? They didn't notice that you hadn't been eating?'

SARAH: 'They've always admired how I looked. Mummy said how lucky I was not to have puppy fat like she did, and she's quite fat now you know.'

THERAPIST: 'If you were to describe your parents so that I could recognize them, how would you do it? Help me build up a picture.'

SARAH: 'As I said, Mummy is overweight. She could be very attractive – I know she was when she was younger as I have seen pictures of her. She's tallish, black hair and dark eyes; she frowns a lot; she works in a doctor's surgery part-time. Daddy, well he's tall and very handsome; keeps his figure – he plays squash regularly; he's a solicitor and very brainy and very charming.'

THERAPIST: 'I'm not sure that I would recognize them. Can you give me more detail? How do they speak; what tone of voice; what do they wear?'

This dialogue continued for some time with Sarah becoming more confident at describing her parents' roles, or more accurately building up a character profile of each of them, including their clothes. I then went on to ask her to describe herself in the same way. Finally I asked her to choose one of the animals to represent each of her parents and herself. She said it was impossible. She couldn't see them as animals; they were people – so I said were there any people in the toys or any story she knew that reminded her of herself and her parents. She immediately said 'Red Riding Hood – it used to be my favourite story and I played it at junior school'.

SARAH: 'Red Riding Hood is such a pretty little girl; blonde, like me. I always thought Daddy was like the woodcutter who rescued Red Riding Hood.'

Teaching point

It was important not to push the idea of the animals when she obviously resisted; however, I was interested that she did not dismiss it as silly play or as being childish. She said that she could not represent her parents as animals although there were a vast number to choose from. I was left with the question, why was the thought of animals so frightening, threatening? Too near the truth? . . .

It would be so easy to attempt interpretations in this first session when the client has shared such a symbolic fairy story. Has she presented a story she thinks will please the therapist, or a story that she genuinely enjoys; or is she, indeed unconsciously, communicating something less innocent? It could be all of these things and the wrong sorts of questions could break the tentative bridge that has started to be built.

As we closed the first session, I suggested that she kept a diary of drawings or pictures or poems or stories that she liked or was drawn to, and that she bring it with her to the session next time. Perhaps she could start with Red Riding Hood?

Sarah did not attend for the second session and after I had written to her she arrived the following week, smiling and full of apology – she had completely forgotten. Anyway, did she really have to come, as she was so much better and everything was so busy. I reiterated the contract we had agreed of four sessions before we made any decisions about the future. She then went on to say that she hadn't done any of the homework I had set her because she was busy, but she had traced a couple of pictures which she liked from a newspaper. She opened a school exercise book and showed me her tracings of the head of the Pope and of a lamb that had been born recently.

SARAH: 'I like them both so much. They are both so . . . so pure . . . and good. I wish I was like that.'
THERAPIST: 'Is Red Riding Hood like that?'
SARAH: 'She tries to be – oh, she tries so hard to be good and pure, but it's no good.'

She begins to look very distressed at this point and her eyes fill with tears, but she fights them back, puts on her smile and says:

SARAH: 'So all she can do is to keep on trying.'
THERAPIST: 'It sounds as if she is having to put a great deal of effort into being pure and good.'
SARAH: 'She does, all the time, she can never stop.'
THERAPIST: 'What would happen if she stopped?'
SARAH: 'That would be the end. All the badness would take over and control her. Oh, I know I'm talking about myself as well as Red Riding Hood, but I really cannot say any more.'
THERAPIST: 'Shall we just talk about Red Riding Hood and her story? How is she now?'
SARAH: 'I'll be OK, but I've some things to tell you and it's such a muddle. No, I will tell you a bit now.'
THERAPIST: 'We only have a very short time now; why don't you tell me how the muddle feels, or maybe you could draw the muddle instead of using words?'

Sarah promptly took a black felt pen and drew round and round and round, thought for a moment, placed her two tracings of the Pope and the lamb in the middle, and then said: 'That's how it feels – black and very messy.' Sarah asked me to keep the picture for her until the next session and left saying that she would definitely come and would not forget.

So much speculation is possible on the above disclosure from the story: the two images and then the black drawing. Sarah's story that she shared the following week was that some years before, when she was about eleven, her father had confided in her that he had a mistress – a very beautiful woman whom he loved in quite a different way from her mother. He told her that he slept with this woman, and when he was out late and said he was playing squash or going to the club, that was where he was. She expressed a range of emotions as she recounted her story; some delight at being trusted with such a grown-up secret; guilt at her mother not knowing; envy of the woman, and her own attempts to be slim and beautiful like her. She was very confused at being told intimate sexual details by her father and with their being whispered to her in such a conspiratorial way.

She then asked to stay in therapy to try and sort out her feelings, and when she came for her next session said in a partly proud and partly scared voice that her periods had started.

We can see from the above example how Sarah undoubtedly had a distorted role-model from her father and probably from her mother as well. It would take many sessions to de-role from the confused roles that Sarah had introjected in relation to her identity as a woman and emergent sexual being. Her way of dealing with the conflicts and guilt was to take total control of her body, thereby suppressing her ovulation but also her feelings, and at the same time to emulate the desirable woman her father loved. She had been unable to deal at such an early age with her father's disclosures to her. They in themselves constituted a form of sexual abuse, and also placed an impossible burden on her in relation to her mother. She was unable to cope with the realization of her fantasy of being so close to her father and yet in reality she wasn't, as he had this other woman.

ROLE AND CHARACTER METHODS

We can see in the case histories of David and Sarah that different 'roles' have been used and they need to be clarified before we proceed. In David's situation he was testing out a new aspect of himself – the part of himself that could make a mess; there was no use made of dramatic distancing of himself in a different role. With Sarah there was a small amount of distancing as she was asked to become her parents[3].

If we look back to Chapter 2, in the story of 'The Magic Forest' there is a dramatization through roles (or characters) without language – this story is told through movement and sound. There is substantial dramatic distancing as the children take on the characters of either the animals or the trees in the magic forest. In this case the roles become the medium for more social interaction and care and trust as well as the development of the imagination.

In Chapter 3, the case history of Trevor again demonstrates both the extension of self as well as the testing of a character. In the toy play in the soft corner Trevor is experimenting with his own strengths as well as testing the therapist; he gives me the role of the silent monster which he is going to kill.

We should look carefully at how this transition from everyday reality to dramatic play reality is made; it is always a progression from earlier work – either in embodiment or projection – which naturally leads into participation in role. Sometimes, as with Trevor, there is an immediate request for role work, both for himself and the therapist. *Dramatic play can be said to be at its most fulsome and effective when the therapist and child are both engaged in imaginary characters.*

Some playtherapists, however, although they feel confortable with projective techniques, feel less at ease with role work. There is no way round this apart from appropriate training in dramatic play, theatre techniques and drama generally. This leads to a greater appreciation of the relationship between the two realities – that of everyday and that of dramatic play.

Although the above examples illustrate how dramatic play emerges from the continuing playtherapy work, the following suggestions are also 'ways in' to stage 3 of the Playtherapy Method.

Projective techniques as starters
Most of the techniques described in Chapter 3 can lead into role work. Pictures, scenes, 'worlds', family groupings, and so on, can go beyond the 'illustration' and become 'inhabited' and 'enacted'.

It may be that the child wants the therapist also in role – it may be that they want the therapist as witness and audience, perhaps even performing the function of chorus and commenting on the play.

Postcards of landscapes
You need a very large collection of picture postcards which include countryside, town, city, valleys, mountains, rivers, seas, gardens, woods, forests, fertile as well as barren and stark images. The child chooses one of these to talk about their life and enacts the scenes that take place in the landscape – as people or creatures of various sorts.

Postcards of people
Again a large collection is needed to provide a spectrum of choices – of different ages, ethnic groups, family, pairs, single people, children of all ages, and so on. In my collection I have many cards from the National Portrait Gallery, London, as well as pictures from the Third World.

Fairy stories and myths
Just as Sarah, earlier in this chapter, talked about Red Riding Hood, there are many stories with which children readily identify and would like to participate in – the following list is a brief resumé of stories that both children and adolescents have asked for:

- The Three Bears
- The Laidley Worm
- Jack and the Beanstalk

- Alice in Wonderland
- The Snow Queen
- The Three Billy Goats Gruff
- The Three Little Pigs
- Beauty and the Beast

These stories may be told and enacted during the telling or enacted after the telling; the endings may be changed if the child so wishes. Different roles may be experienced so that the child expands his or her own perception and role repertoire.

SUMMARY

In this chapter we have seen the importance of role development (stage 3 in the EPR developmental paradigm) in early childhood and how its roots lie in the imitative play of babies. Several examples have shown how inappropriate role-modelling can disable a child from healthy development and relationships, and how the use of different forms of dramatic play can bring about change.

NOTES

[1]   There are many reports of children living in nature – wolf children, children in battery cages, and the stories of Romulus and Remus, Mowgli and Greystoke. The *New York Times* of 24 February 1985 reported that Ramu, a young Indian boy had been found some years before, reportedly reared by wolves. He was taken to Mother Teresa's Centre. According to Gleitman (1986) he preferred a crouch position, continued to eat raw meat, and did not acquire language.

[2]   'It is the time you have wasted for your rose that makes your rose so important.'
'It is the time I have wasted for my rose –' said the little prince, so that he would be sure to remember.
'Men have forgotten this truth' said the fox. 'But you must not forget it. You become responsible, forever, for what you have tamed. You are responsible for your rose. . . .'
'I am responsible for my rose', the little prince repeated, so that he would be sure to remember.
from *The Little Prince* by Antoine de Saint-Exupery.

[3]   Compare with the case history of Eddie (Jennings, 1989).

REFERENCES

Cattanach, A. (1992) *Play Therapy with Abused Children*, pp 34–6. London: Jessica Kingsley.

Courtney, R. (1982) *Re-Play*. Toronto: Oise Press.

De Saint-Exupery, A. (1945; 1982) *The Little Prince*. London: Piccolo.

Dodd, N. & Hickson, W. (1971) *Drama and Theatre in Education*. London; Heinemann Educational.

Edgar, D. (1978) *Mary Barnes: a Play*, Act I, scenes 6 & 7. London: Methuen.

Garvey, C. (1984) *Children's Talk*, pp 187–215. London: Fontana.

Gersie, A. (1991) *Story Making in Bereavement*. London: Jessica Kingsley.

Gersie, A. & King, N. (1990) *Story Making in Education and Therapy*. London: Jessica Kingsley.

Gleitman, H. (1986) *Psychology*. New York: Norton.

Jennings, S. (1989) The Trying Time: Dramatherapy with Adolescents'. In *Special Educational Needs Review*, Vol. 2 (Ed. N. Jones). London: Falmer Press.

Jennings, S. (1990) *Dramatherapy with Families, Groups and Individuals*. London: Jessica Kingsley.

Jennings, S. & Gersie, A. (1987) Dramatherapy and Disturbed Adolescents in *Dramatherapy Theory and Practice* (Ed. S. Jennings), pp 162–82. London: Routledge.

McCaslin, N. (Ed) (1981) *Children and Drama*. New York: Longman.

Von Franz, M. (1987) *The Interpretation of Fairytales*. Dallas: Spring.

Wagner, B.J. (1979) *Dorothy Heathcote: Drama as a Learning Medium*. London: Hutchinson Educational.

Chapter 5

Playtherapy Methods

In the previous three chapters we were concerned with the developmental paradigm of embodiment–projection–role and with basic playtherapy methods that facilitate this process. In this chapter we concern ourselves with a more extensive range of methods for the playtherapist's practice.

SENSORY PLAY

Touch methods

In Chapter 2 we discussed the ambivalence of therapists, teachers and others towards physically touching children. The sad situation we find currently is that many parents also are less spontaneous about touching their children since they are anxious about touch being misinterpreted.

We know, however, that children only develop a body-image through being handled and touched in a variety of ways which include both containment and excitement – the ritual/risk approach that is described in Chapter 7. There is a range of playful methods which allow a child to re-experience healthy experiences of touching and being touched which can form part of a session with an individual child and can then be re-experienced with peers in group sessions.

Rolling methods

In Chapter 2 rolling is described as part of the embodiment process which takes the child through a development of physical maturation from lying to standing (lying, sitting, crawling, standing).

> 'Rolling is a series of falls, the safest the body can do. It involves letting go of weight and giving in to the pull of gravity. Tense, anxious children roll rigidly like a log, with their forearms protecting the chest and the head lifted.'
>
> (Sherborne, 1990: 10)

When the child rolls unaided, he or she is managing the whole body in relation to the floor. The floor contains the child, i.e. you cannot fall off the floor, and the child is receiving continuous feedback in relation to the floor: its temperature, texture, resilience and so on.

When the therapist rolls the child, with the child allowing itself to be rolled (*working with*), touch is involved in a co-operative endeavour, with the child receiving physical signals from the therapist. In the contrasting technique where the child resists being rolled (*working against*), the child is learning to say 'no' through its own body and to develop autonomy. The child's non-verbal signalling system is being understood and its body boundaries are being respected. When the child rolls the therapist, both with and against, the child now has the experience of being in control of the touching, as well as continuing to develop the body-self.

Case history

Clive, aged seven, was referred for playtherapy after being subject to violent outbursts from his stepfather and was very wary, nervous and watchful. He played various versions of the violent episodes with the toys and we then went on to look at how the *toys* could play and 'have fun'. Clive gradually discovered physical games for miniature toys, then for larger figures to play, which were not violent.

Eventually he was ready to respond to the invitation: 'Shall we play together like the toys?' His initial response to the rolling play was to lie on the floor with his eyes screwed up and his whole body very tense. I received this as 'working against' and made an effort to roll him which he resisted, i.e. I translated his tension into an apropriate response within the play, re-framing the experience. As I pushed him I said, 'You're not going to let me roll you; I'm pushing harder . . . but you're still not going to let me . . . good'. I then went on to suggest that he tried to roll me and I would try to stop being rolled over. I stretched out on the floor and he crouched beside me, lightly putting his hands on my side and with his eyes closed tight. I said 'Tell me what you are doing' and he replied 'I'm pushing you . . .', but he kept his eyes closed and I could scarcely feel his hands. 'Push me a bit harder and see if I will roll over. Try to open your eyes to see if you are moving me.' He squinted through his closed eyelids and applied a little more pressure under which I gave way slightly.

It took several sessions for Clive to allow himself to be rolled without anxiety and to resist in a playful way, and conversely to both roll me freely and to try and combat my resistance.

Teaching point

Notice how it was necessary to start with the projective play, that is to distance the child's personal experience of the physical violence through the toys and then to transform that experience, still with toys. Only then was it possible to physically re-frame and re-learn more appropriate touch experiences.

BUILDING A HEALTHY TOUCH REPERTOIRE

We can now re-look at the various physical exercises given in Chapter 2 and consider how they can be used to slowly build up a repertoire of healthy touch experiences for children. These need to be taken in very small steps: the more damaged the child, the more slowly the steps. They are all necessary aspects of the child's transition to healthy playful development.

Texture methods

During normal development, children experience a range of textures from the beginning: soft, smooth, rough, hard, sticky, wet, and so on. Each touch category itself has a range of differentiated experiences that develop very fine 'tuning' in our touch responses. We do not confuse breasts with bottle, even though both may be good to suck. The child's environment is surrounded by a vast range of textures and the following few examples under each category illustrate the extent of touch experience in the early months of life:

- *Human* – hands, breasts, hair, nails, cheeks, lips
- *Clothing/bedding* – wool, cotton, organdie, velvet, satin, embroidery, quilting
- *Food/drink* – milk, juice, water, fruit, purée, rusks
- *Washing/bathing* – water, soap, bubbles, towelling, cream
- *Furniture, etc.* – crib, cot, buggy, pram, bouncer, car seat/door/window, tables, settee
- *Toys/play* – rattle, teddybear, bell, mirror, ball, knitted animal, book

Here, the infant is able to explore touch and texture – principally through the hand and mouth – but also with the remainder of the body. The child who is deprived of, or who has had inappropriate touch experience, needs to be able to re-discover different textures within the play experience. All equipment and materials in the playtherapy room (see Chapter 9) in themselves provide many textures; however, it is also useful to have *structured textured play* as a specific method of working.

Texture boxes and feely bags

The importance of containers such as boxes, bowls, trays and bags is emphasized in order to set limits and boundaries to the child's experience. Boxes and bags which close are useful for indicating the beginning and the end of a sequence and to allow as much exploration as the child can bear.

The texture box

This can be textured – carved, or covered in material or stickers – and thus provide a tactile focus before it is even opened. Inside the box should be a selection of objects of contrasting textures, such as *velvet, sandpaper, eggshells, twigs, shells* and *wool*. These can be explored with eyes closed or open and perhaps with words associated with them. Likes and dislikes can be described, and a story evolved around the contrasting materials.

Example of texture-play from a four-year-old

'The cat stroked its fur (velvet) and then went scritchy-scratchy (sandpaper) on the floor which was cold . . . and . . . nice . . . (shell). It didn't like the sticky mess (eggshell) so had a wash. . . .'

This child is able to differentiate between textures and attempts to add words to communicate the whole experience. The child's distaste for sticky things is expressed in the story through the character of the cat. Later, in sand and water play, the child was able to discover some delight in messy experience, but was always concerned about being clean and tidy to go home.

While experimenting with texture play, start with a small number of things to feel which can develop in complexity. The child itself can also create a texture box of nice and nasty things.

The feely bag

This should also be made of textured material and contain a range of 'touch' objects, such as *orange, small toy, wooden spoon, glove, marble, toy tree, nailbrush*.

The child and therapist take it in turns to choose an object and describe and guess what it is with eyes closed. Pleasant and unpleasant sensations can be described and, again, this can lead into individual or shared storytelling.

The above may seem a variation of very simple games which are a part of normal experience and indeed is similar to some adult party games. Why should it be included in the playtherapist's repertoire and what is its value therapeutically? Some of the benefits are as follows:

- It allows the child to re-discover a range of touch that may be absent or distorted
- This in itself will enable a greater range of expression and communication
- This in turn will allow for greater accessibility to the child's inner life and world experience
- This acts like a 'loop system': the more the child is enabled to play, the more it can access and transform experience
- Thus, therapeutic expression and the further development of play ability are mutually enhancing and beneficial

Teaching point

It is of the greatest importance that the playtherapist is sensitive to and trained to understand the timing and pace of the interventions being described in this chapter. Bombardment with too much stimulus or failure to pick up a child's response can result in major setbacks in therapeutic growth.

Taste, smell, sight, hearing methods

Together with touch, all the above make up the area known as *sensory play* which forms the multi-dimensional aspects of the playtherapy experience. Children who are organically damaged or have the senses impaired through early experience need appropriate stimulation of their potential sensory self. Therefore, play and games which involve all or some of the senses need to be developed. Playing at tea-parties using real or imaginary food, washing and drying dolls, hide-and-seek, tip-toe games, for example, all involve the senses. The playtherapist may create his or her own stories, or use existing fairytales or myths to bring in sensory experience. One example, using the 'Oseo story,' is described below.

Just as the texture box provides a useful starting point, one can also create a *sense box* which contains small items to stimulate the senses. A variety of sense boxes created by a group of playtherapy trainees for use in their practice is described below:

- *Plastic sweet jar* – filled with small polystyrene balls which in turn contain a squeaker, a whistle, wrapped sweets, a lavender bag. This creates a sensory 'lucky dip' with the polystyrene creating an unusually warm texture.
- *Carved wooden box* – (such as sold at charity shops) containing chocolate mints, a bell, a perfume sample, a small spinning top, Velcro.
- *Velvet-lined box* – containing chocolate nuts-and-raisins, a handcream sample, an holograph, a small rattle.

Such sense boxes can be explored in themselves or can lead into other sorts of play and storymaking. Again, a child can create a sense box on either a miniature or a large scale. Both texture and sense boxes are useful introductions to the *journey box* described later in this chapter.

MEDIA FOR SENSORY PLAY

Useful substances for sensory play

The use of the handcream sample listed in one of the sensory boxes leads me into a consideration of a whole range of substances that can be used in playtherapy, primarily to develop or express touch sensation, but also to activate other senses and to provide the context to imaginative play:

- *Body creams* – small samples of hand/face/massage cream are useful for stimulating touch and smell and for a child to allow touch to take place. The cream acts as an intermediary between the therapist and the child; when cream is massaged into the hands, for example, and the child is also able to massage the therapist's hands and then his or her own. All of this touching will develop body-self and image and reinforce the re-framing that is taking place.
- *Play slime* – green slime that slides around and needs 'capturing' to put back into its container can be used both in sensory play and also as a way of expressing 'messy' experiences. The colour, texture and movement of the slime are very powerful and both intrigue and repel the child. It can also be used to express disgust and uncontrolled mess and can serve to articulate experiences that are not easily put into words.
- *Plasticine and Playdoh* – both can be used purely for sensory stimulation of touch and smell. (I know at least one adult who was taken back by the smell of 'original' Plasticine into a vivid recollection of childhood experiences.)
- *Clay* – provides a quite different sensation; colder and less elastic. With additional water, the range of stimuli can be increased.
- *Play pastry* – allow a child to assist with the making of the pastry rather than providing it ready-made. Play pastry can be coloured with powder-colour.

Teaching point

The above substances should be explored in themselves. Too often playtherapists want to urge the child to 'make' something, rather than allowing for the exploratory time. In Chapter 6 on playtherapy with learning-disabled and handicapped children, staff had actually to be instructed to 'create nothing' out of Plasticine in order for the anxiety about getting it right to diminish. Children and staff feel under enormous pressure to 'do the right thing' as if there is only one answer, rather than feeling safe and confident enough to take the risk of exploring. (This can happen with all forms of play – not just with modelling clay.)

Why is the exploratory time so important? Again, the child who has had the opportunity to explore a range of media will be able to communicate more effectively both in the therapy and in ordinary life. Unless a child spontaneously starts to create a scene or image from its own experience through media, the playtherapist should allow for the initial discovery to take place. Cattanach (below) puts this very well:

'I always bring a variety of play dough and tactile material for modelling, smelling and touching and some jelly-like sticky worms and sticky balls which can be touched, ripped up and generally used in whatever way the children think fit.'

(Cattanach, 1992: 64)

Again, caution must be exercised with the use of the above. For the child who is suffering from major trauma, many of these substances can evoke the actual recall of the trauma. For example, substance exploration can be a reminder of sexual abuse and the feelings of mess, stickiness, smell. The child who has experienced violence in relation to food may well become fearful with substances that are similar.

Case history

Jane was taken into care at the age of three with severe bruising on the face, shoulders and arms, and blisters around her mouth. Feeding-time had always proved to be fight-time when both parents attempted to force-feed her. Part of the problem was that she was being fed inappropriate food for her age: 'She should have everything that we have', was the parents' belief and they were increasingly frustrated that she was unable to completely feed herself or that she took a long time. Violence had built up over some time as one parent held her and the other forced food indiscriminately into her. It culminated in an episode when the forced-feeding had ended up with hot food being thrown at her.

In playtherapy Jane was terrified to be near or catch sight of the dolls' house or tea-set and any substances used for playing. She spent a great deal of time testing the environment and the playtherapist for safety and then wanted to spend her initial sessions in the 'soft area' (see Chapter 9). Her next step was to want to draw and crayon sitting at a table. This eventually led to a re-enactment, through small toys, of the violent incidents. Much later there was chance for reparative work on her early physical experiences, through which it was necessary to explore the embodiment stage very fully.

Teaching point

This case history illustrates the supreme importance of starting where the child needs to begin rather than where the play-therapist wants to start. This child was able to give very clear signals of where she needed to work first – through creating and testing a trustful environment. Her next play activity using drawing and crayons was non-messy and under her complete control.

THE IMPORTANCE OF SCALE

Smaller, and much-smaller-than-I-am toys

Most of the play methods described so far are with materials that are smaller than the child and therefore represent the child's real or fantasy world in miniature. A word of caution, however, needs to be introduced here: *what seems miniature to the adult may only seem a little bit smaller to the child. Therefore, we need to provide materials that are smaller and very much smaller when measured against the actual physical size of the child.*

When working with different dimensions of media smaller than itself, the child is able to exercise autonomy and control; also, the smaller the media, the more private the experience. Some children are unable to deal with experiences that for many of us would seem 'life-size', and even the larger toys in the playtherapy room can be quite overwhelming. Many distressed children can experience life on an epic scale that has gone out of control. Hence my emphasis on work in miniature. All of the projective techniques described in Chapter 3 are played with small-scale materials that are generally available in most toyshops. They can be arranged, put away, thrown away, re-assembled, put safely inside boxes, buried in the sand, and so on. Since I am a great believer in the magic and mystery of play, I also provide small toys inside small containers. These can be used for exploration and the chance to find a new way of looking at an issue, or for the sheer magic of discovery in itself. The following are some of the 'miniatures' I use, see also Fig. 5.1; none of them more than two inches in size:

Fig. 5.1 'Miniatures' in a box.

- Punch and Judy with the dog and baby
- Noah's Ark with several minute animals
- 'The Old Woman who Lived in a Shoe'
- Baby dragon emerging from an egg
- Guatemalan worry dolls
- A jester holding a jester on a stick

Many of these toys already come in small boxes and there are trinket tins and boxes that can be acquired to contain the others. They form part of what I call 'the pocket therapist', described in detail in Chapter 8. They are small enough to explore safely an experience that has been too large to cope with, the Punch and Judy and the Old Woman are of particular value here. For other children they become something special that can be discovered as a surprise in a dreary or painful world. What is important is that they are 'good quality' – i.e. that they are not only functional but well made, stimulating and well cared for. This is a theme I shall return to later in this book.

Larger-than-I-am toys

Years ago I heard Bruno Bettelheim talk about the large stone statues he had in the surroundings of his treatment centre. In particular, he drew his audience's attention to a larger-than-lifesize seated naked woman with ample breasts. The children who attended the centre, he said, would play spontaneously with this stone mother and scrub or paint her breasts, curl up in her lap, and, on occasion, stub their toes by kicking her. This also reminded me of the large bronze statues of various Shakespeare characters in the rose gardens at Stratford-upon-Avon. Hamlet's lap is impossible to sit on unless you are a small child, but Falstaff, tankard in one hand, provides an ample lap for an adult of any proportion to sit on and fantasize about uncle, grandfather or even lover.

In work with children, just as it is important to work in media smaller than the child – as well as in the miniature as described above – it is also important to balance these experiences by providing the possibility for working in a media larger than oneself. All playtherapy trainees are required, as part of their training, to make a soft toy that is at least half as large as themselves, as an adult. The first group of trainees to attempt this found that it became a very therapeutic exercise. They all chose animals or characters that

Fig. 5.2 Dr Mooli Lahad with the first trainees in the Playtherapy Method, with the toys they created that were half their own size.

they would have liked for themselves and created them from fabric and textures they found pleasurable. The group (shown in Fig. 5.2) made a badger, whale, donkey, clown, beagle, pearly-king and a leopard.

For the trainees the making of these toys proved a reminder of the frustration of struggling with manipulative skills they had not used for years. As the toys took shape, the playtherapist trainees became even more creative: the donkey had panniers which contained a range of playtherapy materials such as sense bags and its harness was embroidered with different cosmic symbols; the whale was able to 'give birth' to a baby whale. Thus, a group of adults re-created for themselves the equivalent of longed-for transitional objects (see Chapter 1) which, in turn, they were able to use in playtherapy application. Larger-than-life toys, teddybears and dolls, can be bought if not made and are part of the 'soft area' for children to cuddle up to, tussle with, and generally relate to, in both play and stories.

Although the larger-than-I-am toys so far described relate to the soft and cuddly and furry, larger-than-life experiences may need to be played through in a variety of ways. Just as the stone statue could be both a container and something to bruise a toe on, we need to provide things in the environment that have this kind of

reality – i.e. things have their limits. In such cases it is possible to
be hurt, break things, get messy, spill stuff and have castles fall
down. We need to bear this in mind when creating the playtherapy
space, otherwise it could become like the oversafe playpen of
Bobby (see Chapter 2) which resulted in stunted development and
damaged relationships.

Children individually and in groups may also want to build
something that is larger than themselves. Twins – a brother and a
sister – asked to create a 'Dick Monster'. They had worked projectively with the monster toys and in the sandtray – attacking and
burying monsters – and they had drawn different sizes of monster
– both individually and together. It was important that they had
firm boundaries as they entered and left the reality of the play –
the symbolic killing of the monster had to be established with no
guilt that they might actually kill off the abusing parent. It was also
important to place the monster in the context of a dramatized story
so that it became possible to have some resolution before the
playtherapy sessions came to a close. The scenario was as follows:

> 'Once upon a time there was a Dick Monster who hurt all the baby
> dragons in the wood; the lorry came to catch him and took him to
> prison and all the baby dragons grew big and strong and weren't
> frightened anymore.'

The story was to be enacted over three sessions:

(1) *Preparation*: creating the scene, building the monster making
    the magic wand for the man in the lorry
(2) *Dramatization*: the monster in the wood and all the babies
    being frightened and hiding in the trees
(3) *Dramatization*: the capture of the monster and being taken to
    prison; the babies growing up and not being frightened.

The monster was built out of large plastic bags stuffed with
paper, with balloons blown up for facial and genital features. The
absorption during the building and creation was intense, and it
appeared that the creation of a larger-than-life figure was an
important stage in the acknowledgement of the twins' experience –
it seemed to make it concrete for them and for the therapist, as
well as enabling them to be in control. The capture of the monster
involved jumping on it by surprise and the balloons being burst

and a lot of trampling and stamping. Then the bedraggled remains were taken away and the baby dragons had a 'safe party'.

Teaching point

In the above example the therapist takes the cues from the children but is alert enough to provide the appropriate structures of the story and to institute the three sessions time management. By asking the children to tell the story – however short – it is possible, as in this example, to reach some kind of resolution. Note how the monster was deflated and controlled but not totally destroyed.

'Whereas psychotherapists will recall particular theorists . . . or case histories; dramatherapists recall themes from dramatic works of art – plays performances, myths, images, metaphors and symbols.'
(Jennings, 1990; 100)

I cannot emphasize too strongly the importance of maintaining the play reality boundaries as described in the above example. At one point the boy of the pair asked if he could take the monster to the woods and attack it there – this would have confused the boundaries and would not have had a healing effect.

Containers that I can fit inside

A lot of play equipment is now designer-made and leaves little scope for the flexibility and imagination of the child. Many children gain more from a blanket draped over a table than they do from an expensive Wendy house. Large cardboard boxes (such as those which contain freezers or televisions); large paper sacks, blankets and large nesting boxes are all necessary for what I term 'container play'. Children in therapy often need more than just the safety of the playtherapy room and the playtherapist; they want to create a space within the space where they can hide, talk from, or create stories or dramas. Some children may spend a long time under the blankets in the soft corner, re-creating a safe bed.

All of these situations need to be brought into the play themes as part of the continuing story; for example, if a certain box becomes the cupboard in which the child used to be locked, it becomes a frightening place within the play. At the end of the play it needs to be de-roled and returned to being just a box. Whatever the media, they become a part of the play experience for the duration of the play, and then become neutral. If the child wants to dramatize scenes or stories that have frightening overtones, make sure that there is also a safe place to return to. The whole room may, for example, be turned into an environment for the drama with the 'soft' corner a safe place where monsters cannot invade and where the ground is firm and does not swallow people up.

Container toys

I have already described boxes and other containers that hold toys and objects and materials that are large enough to contain the child. There are also other toys which are made up as something inside something, inside something else which have particular playtherapy methods associated with them. The best known is the Russian Babushka doll where several peasant women, carved in wood, are contained one within the other down to a very small size. The dolls are usually at least five in number and may be many more. Children and adults are captivated by these dolls and may spend much time examining and arranging them in different ways. There are several ways of using Babushka:

- To explore the dynamics of the members of the family
- To externalize the different people the child feels are inside itself
- To create the ideal family: 'how I would like it to be'
- To explore issues around new babies and siblings
- To tell stories with, the dolls providing the starting point

Playtherapists will find that children spontaneously make use of Babushka in many different ways, often guiding a therapist through a scene.

Case history

Mary had taken all the dolls out from the Babushka and had stood them in a group. She examined each, talking to herself as she did so, 'Hmmm, this is a fat one, it must be the mother; this is auntie and she and mummy have a row . . . the little girl starts to cry so her big sister takes her to play outside . . . the auntie goes home because she is crying . . . and mummy cooks the tea. . . .'

During this time, Mary moved the dolls around as if they were puppets and the grouping of four dolls went from being altogether to the two smaller ones being placed at one end of the table, the 'aunt' under the table, and the 'mother' at the other end. It was only then that I realized that Mary was playing with four Bahushkas and that the smallest was nowhere to be seen. I gave a gentle prompt and said, 'What happens then?'

As if I hadn't spoken, Mary continued her story:

'The fat mummy has got to go into hospital so she has to call the auntie back again . . . come here stupid woman . . . you must look after these children . . . the ambulance is coming. . . .'

She brought the 'aunt' back again who called the children in from the garden and gave them tea, and they waved to mummy who was going to hospital.

'The mummy went to the hospital to have a baby . . . the baby was dead . . . so mummy came home without it . . . and she and the auntie both cried.'

She took the smallest Babushka from inside the large one:

'The baby's got to be buried.'

She fetched some sand in a small plastic bowl.

'You must be buried because you're dead.'

She picked up two small dolls and said:

'. . . and the girls cry because the baby is dead and they haven't got a new sister.'

She looked up and said:

'That's the end.'

This was a multi-layered statement for a small child dealing with a bereavement that had not been explained to her.

The baby had died within minutes of birth and the mother had 'dealt' with everything at the hospital before she had returned home. She did not think it important for the two daughters to be involved in the brief funeral service and had not shared anything with her children.

PLAYING OUT THE TRAUMATIC EXPERIENCE

Monsters

Every playtherapy room needs sufficient monster toys, such as dinosaurs and science-fiction toys to enable children to play out the frightening scenes they have experienced – and to re-create them and control them. There are some actual terrors that children have to overcome which must be distinguished from the healthy 'scarey' play most children delight in. Games of surprise starting with 'Peep-Bo' for infants illustrate how children seek situations that have increasing fear and excitement – provided that in the end the situation can be coped with, or the child can be rescued. The actor Donald Sinden, while playing Mr Darling and Captain Hook in J.M. Barrie's 'Peter Pan', said that it was obvious they were one and the same person. He took great pains to be still distinguishable as Mr Darling while playing Captain Hook – as he said, it was really father dressing up and pretending to be the wicked captain.

However, when play breaks the boundaries of play rules and becomes part of the lived reality, the child becomes confused and terrorized. The example of the 'I'm coming to get you' case history in Chapter 3 aptly illustrates the abuse of play.

Monsters can be made with Plasticine or clay, drawn or painted, or enacted in stories and dramas. Many storybooks have monster stories which can be read or dramatized. Perhaps one of the best examples of a monster becoming something other than frightening is the song of 'Puff the Magic Dragon'.

The story of Oseo

The Oseo story is based on a North-American tale and is a firm favourite with groups and individuals of all ages. Ideally, since it lends itself to being dramatized as it is told, the playtherapist can join in as the story is told, whether with an individual or a group. The text of the Oseo story appears below. As you read it through slowly, be aware of the following:

- The story starts and ends in the safe place
- It involves a ritual control factor (stop, look, listen)
- Participants are involved in physically overcoming the elements (climbing over/under/through)
- A wide range of physical movement is required as well as physical control
- The giant provides the monster larger-than-life
- The child/hero is able to problem-solve
- The child/hero cares for others (bird and squirrel)
- The child/hero is helped by others
- The consequence of rule-breaking is realized
- There is a successful outcome even though the monster is frightening and in control

The story should start with the playtherapist setting the scene and the child/children sitting cross-legged in their imaginary wigwams, whittling away at a piece of wood. During the pauses the children fill in with suitable noises, actions and words. Although the story is originally about a young boy it can be adapted as the therapist sees fit. It begins:

'Oseo was an Indian boy who lived in a village very near the forest. He was always getting into scrapes and had far more adventures than all the other children.

One day he was sitting in his wigwam carving a piece of wood with his sheath knife . . . and wondering how to stop being bored. He decided to go and explore a new forest path so he jumped up, put on his jacket with the secret pockets, his special shoes which are called . . . , and crept quickly and quietly out of his tent, over the fence and into the dark forest.

Although mischievous, Oseo always remembered the forest code, that whenever he heard a noise he must stop, look and listen because it could be something dangerous. He went on down the path whistling to himself, wondering where it would lead, and suddenly he heard a loud screech. So he . . . yes, he stopped, looked and listened. . . . But it was only the magic hoola bird flying away in the treetops so Oseo went on his way.

The path got narrower and narrower and creepers began to get in his way. Soon he was pushing through the undergrowth, over fallen logs . . . clambering over boulders . . . and hacking his way through shrubs and bushes with his pocket knife. He came to a clearing and sat down for a rest under a large tree. He noticed a tiny bird at the foot of the tree and looked up and saw it must have fallen out of its nest. He gently picked it up, stretched on tiptoe and just managed to put it back.

He was just going when the mother bird came to the edge of the nest and said "Don't go Oseo, I've got a surprise for you. You've been very kind to me." Oseo stretched up his hand wondering what it could be and was a little disappointed when the bird put a small dried pea into his palm, but she said, "Take good care of this because it's magic." So Oseo put it in his secret pocket and went on his way.

He followed the path again and had to jump across several ditches. Suddenly he heard a strange whirring sound, so he . . . stopped, looked and listened . . . but it was only a rattlesnake which slid away into the undergrowth and did not trouble him. He came to the banks of a river and was wondering how to get across when he saw a squirrel sitting by the water crying. Oseo asked him what the matter was and the squirrel said that he wanted to cross the river but couldn't swim. Oseo said, "That's all right, you can sit on my head and I will take you across." He carefully lifted the squirrel, placed him on his head and began to wade into the water. It was very cold and came up to his ankles, then his knees, then his tummy, then his feet couldn't feel the bottom and he began to swim to the other side. He stepped out of the water and put the squirrel down. He squeezed his clothes dry and jumped up and down to get warm again. Meanwhile the squirrel had disappeared and then came back and said, "You've been very good to me Oseo, I want to give you a present." Oseo held out his hand and the squirrel gave him an acorn. He was very disappointed but the squirrel said, "It's magic, Oseo, keep it with you and it might help you one day." Oseo said goodbye, climbed up a grassy bank and over a fence into a large field.

He was running around in the grass feeling very happy and suddenly heard "Ehhhhaahhhhhhhhh". He stopped, looked and listened and saw the most enormous giant coming towards him, "Ehhhhaahhhhhhhhh". Oseo began to run but the giant was getting nearer and bellowed "I'm going to catch you, Oseo, for my dinner tonight" and he threw a huge net over him. Oseo struggled and struggled but the net got tighter and tighter and more and more tangled and he couldn't move at all. The giant stomped off saying he was going to fetch a cooking pot. Oseo felt very sad and knew he would never see his village again and started to cry. Then he remembered the bird's present – he managed to get one hand free to get the magic pea out of his secret pocket. He put it on the end of his tongue, closed his eyes and wished very very hard, and sure enough he began to get smaller, and smaller, until he was so small that he was able to climb out through one of the holes in the net.

Oseo began to run towards the river and heard the giant coming in the background. All the grass felt like an enormous forest and was prickling his legs and scratching him. Tiny pebbles seemed like great big rocks. He got to the fence and lay on his tummy and wriggled underneath, rolled down the bank and stood by the river realising he was too small to get across. The giant was getting nearer – what could he do? Yes . . . the acorn. He got it out of his secret pocket, put it on the end of his tongue, closed his eyes and wished very hard. Sure enough he began to grow bigger and bigger until he was back to his normal size again.

Oseo dashed into the river, swam as fast as he could to the other side, didn't wait to dry himself and started running along the path. He came to the clearing, sprinted across it and then came to the hard bit where he had to fight his way through the undergrowth. Everything got in his way but at last he got through and there was the path again leading to the camp. He got to the fence and very quietly climbed over, went to his wigwam and gave a sigh of relief. He took off his Indian jacket, put his moccasins by the door and sat down cross-legged on the floor. He began whittling his piece of wood again and thinking about his big adventure; but when anyone came past his tent they would never have thought anything had happened.'

The journey box

The story of Oseo gives us the opportunity to enact a journey of adventure and danger with successful outcome and resolution. To close this chapter, here is another container method that enables the child to tell the difficult journey or to find new resources for the future. The journey box can be created by the playtherapist (there can be several amongst the equipment and the child can choose one), or the child/children can create a box for themselves.

Use a shoebox or similar as the container and inside create a landscape which has varied flora and fauna. The landscape may be made from a combination of the following: card, paper, fabric, cellophane, paint, leaves, twigs. Include the following: mountains, water, forest, paths, and so on.

The journey box acts as a prompt to enable a child to get into the metaphorical journey of past, present and future and develop a language of images. The journey box *contains* the journey, however difficult or frightening the child's experience has been, and is small enough to allow a child to deal with those episodes: children readily grasp the use of landscape and journey to articulate their experiences. The child may start with a ready-made box and then experiment with his or her own box. Always create an interesting 'outside' to the box with paint or stick-ons, and make sure that the lid is firmly closed afterwards.

The creation of the landscape inside the box may be compared with the Lowenfeld techniques where the child creates its world in the sand with a range of toys and objects. The journey box (or the texture or sense or story boxes) may be used pre-Lowenfeld when a child needs to have its experience contained. For some children, the vastness of a sandbox can be too much in the early stages. Remember what was said earlier in the chapter about playing in miniature and the idea of 'the pocket therapist'.

These boxes are all means of transition into the metaphoric and symbolic world of the child, through which an expansion of play can take place. Work with journey boxes can progress into enacted dramawork as situations and scenes develop and children become ready to dramatize through characters and roles.

SUMMARY

This chapter has described a range of developed methods which mainly focus on embodiment and projection with some work on enacted scenes and stories. We might call this progression 'from roll-play to role-play'. I have tried to emphasize the importance of a range of dimensions to the play which is a particular feature of the Playtherapy Method; dimensions such as 'smaller than I am', 'larger than I am' make it possible for the child to re-work the experience in the way that feels right.

Summary of techniques to promote use of the senses

- *Touch*: rolling with and against; safety and texture of the floor; learning to say 'no' with the body
- *Projective rolling*: with toys for the anxious child
- *Texture play*: texture box and feely bag
- *Taste, smell, sight, hearing*: the sense box, substances and creams, slime, modelling clay, pottery clay
- *Smaller and much smaller than I am*
- *Larger than I am*
- *Container play*: that children can get into
- *Container play*: that contains various toys and objects
- *Monsters*
- *The story of Oseo*
- *Journey box*

REFERENCES

Cattanach, A. (1992) *Playtherapy with Abused Children*. London: Jessica Kingsley.

Jennings, S. (1973) *Remedial Drama*. London: A & C Black.

Jennings, S. (1990) *Dramatherapy with Families, Groups and Individuals*. London: Jessica Kingsley.

Sherborne, V. (1990) *Developmental Movement for Children*. Cambridge: Cambridge University Press.

Chapter 6

Playtherapy with Children with Learning Disabilities

In this chapter I want to deal with the special needs of learning-disabled children and to stress the importance of play and play-therapy in all stages of their development. Many assumptions are made about such children's ability to play, especially those children who suffer from severe learning disabilities. Play is a means of learning – most especially it is a means of expressing thoughts and feelings. I emphasize 'expression' because the child with severe learning disabilities will have a limited range of communication pathways. On the one hand intellectual development is retarded and the child has limited ability to communicate through concept and language; on the other hand the child's affective experience – the whole range of emotion and feeling – is as powerful as that of a non-disabled child. This latter child, however, has many ways of communicating – especially through the different nuances of language.

Many disabled children have been deprived of early play experience, either through hospitalization and the results of institutionalization, or through ambivalence or rejection or even ignorance on the part of parents and professionals in the child's early universe. As an example of this, one such professional, talking to the distressed parents of a recently delivered Down's Syndrome baby, said, 'of course you will have a lot of fun with him – Down's are born actors and are always happy!'

There is no doubt that most Down's children and adults do have a ready capacity to mimic and entertain, but this tends to overshadow their other emotional needs and the expression of feelings. Also I have come across frequent 'indulgence' of Down's children (which they readily exploit!) where they are allowed to push unacceptable limits of behaviour and then charm their way out when parents or nurses become exasperated.

There is continuing pressure on society to address the needs of all disabled people in relation to their artistic provision (Lord, 1981). Several professional theatre companies have been formed in the UK with disabled actors; at least two of these groups, Strathcona and Kaleidoscope[1], have actors who have severe learning disabilities. This illustrates how attitudes towards arts and disabilities are beginning to change (Attenborough Report, see Lord, 1985), and also how the skills and talents of severely learning disabled people can be maximized. These theatre companies demonstrate that all participants, whether disabled or not, can belong to a professional artistic world which can be judged by professional standards. Perhaps if there was far *more* theatre and drama in all spheres of our lives, there would be less need for play- and dramatherapists.

I do not want to get into the debate of whether we should refer to 'play' or to 'playtherapy'. I do not look upon the word therapy as having a pejorative connotation since much of the practice described with children with severe learning disability is the play of *repair*, I am content not to separate out these two overlapping areas.

PRINCIPLES OF WORKING WITH CHILDREN WITH LEARNING DISABILITIES

Most of the methodology already described in the early chapters of this book is also appropriate for application with learning-disabled people; in fact many of the ideas originated in work with children with very severe disabilities, particularly the work of Sherborne (1975), Heathcote (1981) and my own work described in *Remedial Drama* (1973). Most of the work outlined in this book is based on the extensive remedial play and drama developed at Anstalt Wittekindshof, a large 2000-bed hospital for people of all ages (from babies to elderly people) with severe learning disability in Westphalia, Germany, and also a similar but smaller institution, at Hendrik van Bouijon Oord in Assen, Holland. With another pioneer in this field, Gordon Wiseman, I made several visits to both centres to establish a training and a practice programme.

We were able to demonstrate that even the person with multiple disabilities is able to contribute to a session of dramatic play. We worked especially with children with distressing stereotyped movements such as rocking, head banging and 'flicking', often with accompanying cries and moans. In these cases, often the child is punished for the behaviour or medication is increased. However, we were able to show that there *is* an alternative approach – these movements and sounds can be considered isolated and isolating ritual expression which it is possible to integrate into shared rhythmic movement and sound. This takes time and a slow, step-by-step building process. However, when a severely autistic child was able to sustain a small group rhythm, hospital staff became convinced that dramatic play had potential.

Teaching point

1. Do not assume that because a child has a learning disability he or she is unable to develop and use imagination.
2. Do encourage all the playing and creativity that is possible at every stage of the day.

If you are starting to practise playtherapy then try to build on the structures that already exist in your hostel, centre or hospital[2]. For example, at Wittekindshof, the children hold hands and sing a 'good morning' song before they eat their meal; it was thus possible to build on that culture and lead into singing games and then more developed play. The children were also able to teach me because I do not speak German so it became a two-way process.

I was quite unable to deal with the total collapse into laughter that overcame one young group with whom we were improvising a journey on a bus into the countryside – I was the bus driver and we were commenting on what we could see in the countryside. Chairs placed in pairs behind each other formed the bus and we had already bought tickets and climbed aboard. Suddenly I jammed on the brakes and said that we had to stop – 'because we had run over a dog'. I could not understand why there was laughter until I realized that I had said that we had run over a pig! (It was some time later that I realized that the two words for dog and pig had entered my unconscious having seen countless war and spy films where uniformed persons are always calling each other 'Schweinhund'!).

THE DELHI PLAYTHERAPY TRAINING PROGRAMME

What follows is a detailed description of a special training programme conducted in Delhi for people who worked with children with learning disabilities.

Teaching point

The aim of the project was to develop 'hands on' experience with a group of professionals together with their disabled pupils and trainees. This was felt to be particularly important since without involving the children themselves in order to show what is possible, much work gets lost between the teaching and the practice.

The following account of the training course illustrates how the playing and drama itself can open up new insights for the staff in relation to the children with whom they work. I choose this programme for the examples in this chapter because it shows how one can develop a through line of working – that is, one where the sessions are creatively developed and not just a heterogeneous collection of techniques. The first three days were set aside for a group of 40 teachers, nurses, occupational therapists, actors, physiotherapists and speech therapists, who had travelled from all over India. The intention was for them to develop basic skills in playtherapy and dramatherapy. The through line was developed in the following three days when a group of 25 children with learning disabilities ranging from medium to severe, came and worked with the group. The learning could thus become a 'hands on' experience, where the basic learning could be consolidated and tested with the client group. I worked with my daughter, Ros Hickson, who is a voice specialist and theatre director and we decided to co-work as a joint team providing the drama and the therapy.

One major concern was not to superimpose artistic and cultural values from the West on an ancient and culturally very rich society. At one level it was difficult to believe that we could contribute anything to the existing vast plethora of myth and legend, drama and dance. This feeling increased when two of the Catholic nuns on the course who had come from Kerala in the far south described the production they had staged of *The Ramayana* with a large group of people with severe learning disabilities[3].

Day one: introduction

(1) Theory: the EPR developmental paradigm, and its appropriateness with children with learning disabilities.

Embodiment
(a) reinforces the development of body-self and the stimulus for sensory awareness and discrimination.
(b) grounds a child's experience physically and allows other learning to take place (Sherborne, op. cit.).

Projection
(c) provides the means for a child to 'make sense' of images, thoughts and feelings in non-verbal media (e.g. finger-paint, clay, Plasticine, drawing, etc.).
(d) enhances the imagination and encourages the development of symbol and metaphor.

Role
(e) provides the opportunity for children to practise appropriate behaviours which are necessary for their social universe.
(f) leads into character work in dramatic play which enables the child to encounter a whole range of experiences – both positive and negative – which otherwise would not be available (see below where a child was able to be both the captain of the ship and the doctor who gave the painful injections!).

(2) Why use dramatic play?

(a) To energize a group, especially if they have been institutionalized (many people with learning disabilities have become used to long periods of sitting).

(b) To contain unfocused energy and channel it into creative expression.
(c) To provide a means of communication and development for withdrawn children.
(d) To practise developmental sequences of learning in order to reinforce maturation.
(e) To allow the expression of a range of human feelings and emotions.
(f) To provide a basic framework on which to build creative drama and theatre.

It should be noted that in India, developed resources for people with disabilities is still a relatively new concept. The new ideas are being resourced in the main by the voluntary sector.

Practical work

Contact relaxation

This makes use of the four points of contact in order for a child to feel reassurance and relaxation through the playtherapist's own body. Usually the child is sitting on the floor and the leader is kneeling behind. There is contact against the legs of the leader and also against the child's shoulders as well as both hands being rested in the leader's hands. This contact/relaxation exercise provides for a maximum body contact in order to communicate non-verbally.

Large group struggle

The whole group holds hands firmly and tries to pull and struggle in various directions without breaking the circle.

Rolling, sitting and crawling

- roll a partner over and over without resisting, and then, with resisting (introducing the concept of working with a partner and working against a partner – see Chapter 2 and Sherborne, 1990.
- Sit back-to-back with a partner and take turns to push each other across the room, and resist being pushed (as above).

- Crawl on hands and knees and go over or under anybody that you meet. This introduces the concept of over and under. As was stated earlier in this book, these sequences mirror normal human development as well as being a basis for imaginative playing.

Sitting struggle

Allow the child to sit in front of you, putting your arms underneath his or her arms and your legs over his or her legs. The child can safely struggle and, at the same time, feel the reassurance of being contained (Fig. 6.1). It is also a useful technique for a child who has become agitated or hysterical (it also comes under the heading of 'container play').

Standing struggle

- With a partner, face each other and see who can push each other across the room.

Fig. 6.1 Sitting struggle.

- Struggle with a partner and see whose shoulders touch the floor first.
- Holding arms with a partner, try to kick his or her knees (only to be undertaken with bare feet).

These exercises can be developed in threes, with two people holding hands and a third struggling to get in or struggling to get out.

The centre of the body

Curl up with the knees under the chin and slowly open out and then curl up again. This can be done singly or with an adult curled against a child.

The idea of curling up and then opening can be developed in creative exercises such as cats waking up, flowers opening, and so on.

Concentration and co-ordination

In groups of four, one person is the child and the other three choose a different clockwork toy and wrap themselves up in an imaginary parcel. The child opens the parcel and winds up the toys one at a time which then start to walk/march/hop/dance/crawl etc. across the room. It is the child's job to stop the toys bumping into each other or the wall by turning them round.

The balloon exercise

I have written up this exercise in several publications (Jennings 1973; 1986), so I will briefly summarize it here:

The group mime the idea of blowing up a balloon and then, in pairs, one person blows the other person up as a balloon, counts to three, and then bursts it. It can then lead into a group balloon that is blown up and then burst.

This exercise, which is extremely popular with all ages, although seeming simple, actually seeds in several concepts. It develops tension and relaxation; it allows touch; it develops co-operation, and, very importantly, it will demonstrate to the playtherapist whether or not the child can make the step from concrete play to symbolic play.

Day One closed with the group creating a non-verbal story using the theme of balloons.

Day two:

Theory

(1)   The importance of non-verbal communication through body and sound can be summarized as follows.

   (a) Takes the pressure off verbal communication, especially where there may be minimal or no language at all.
   (b) Legitimizes touch and enables relationships to develop.
   (c) Moves away from the hierarchical to the more democratic and collaborative relationship.
   (d) By developing the body and voice we maximize the expressive potential of the child.

(2)   Playing games:

   (a) Games can be collaborative or competitive, and both are important.
   (b) Basic playground games can be developed in a variety of ways.
   (c) Children enjoy the ritual and repetitive nature of games.
   (d) Games encourage co-operation, co-ordination and memory.

(3)   Using the story structure to develop the imagination:

   (a) Stories with a beginning, middle and end provide a structure for playing within which the child can develop the imagination.
   (b) Within the story, the child can experience a range of emotions and events, which further develop his or her capacities.

Practical work

The rain-maker exercise

Everyone sits in a circle on the floor and rubs their hands together and, at a given signal, slaps their thighs and then drums their fingers on the floor. When this is done in a large group, it sounds like very heavy rain which then tails off. This idea can be played with in various ways and done like a non-verbal 'round' to improve concentration.

Standing up one-at-a-time

This exercise is much harder than it looks and it will usually take several attempts before it gets anywhere near succeeding. Children tend to be much better at it than adults. Everybody sits in a big circle on the floor and people have to get up one at a time. If two people get up together, then everybody has to sit down and start again. It gets most frustrating when nineteen people have stood up and then the twentieth and twenty-first get up together. It is an excellent game for concentration and awareness of others.

The four tasks

Select four simple tasks for the group to complete, such as:

(1) March up and down on the spot ten times
(2) Touch the floor with the flat of the hand
(3) Sing the first verse of a well-known song (one that is appro-
     priate for age and culture)
(4) Complete the sentence 'Play is. . . .'

The real task of this exercise lies in synchrony. First of all, two pairs do the four tasks exactly together; then fours, eights, and so on, until the whole group has completed the tasks at exactly the same time. The group leader needs at least two helpers to monitor the exactness and the whole exercise both provides a lot of fun and emphasizes the importance of practising accuracy. It also looks at leadership issues since, once the group gets bigger, different individuals try to 'conduct' the group, and nothing is more in-furiating than a self-appointed leader who then marches eleven times instead of ten.

Circle games

Ask everybody to make circles as follows:

(1) A random circle where they are aware of who is on either side
     of them.

(2)   A circle that is based on their height from tall to short.
(3)   A circle that is based on age.
(4)   A circle that is based on food preferences.

During the course of this exercise call out (as appropriate) 'Circle One', 'Circle Four', etc., and everybody then has to remember their particular place in that circle.

Number games

The simplest number game involves calling out a number and people have to form groups of that number. Not only does this reinforce numeracy, it also develops concentration.

A more complex number game consists of allotting numbers to different body parts. Feet and knees, for example, can count one each; hands count ten; bottoms count five. Groups of five people then have to see if they can only have four points on the floor. This game can be made more or less difficult, depending on the ability of the group.

The magic forest

The story of the lost animals sheltering in the forest is told in Chapter 2. The description given here was carried out with a mixed group of children with learning disabilities.

Voice work

The importance of correct breathing

The most useful method to teach is intercostal–diaphragmatic or rib reserve breathing. The diaphragm is supported by the tenacity of the abdominal muscles, and the ribs are expanded and the diaphragm pushed down as the lungs fill with air. For a detailed description, see Cicely Berry (1975) where she gives a range of breathing exercises as well as voice practice.

Correct breathing is important for the child to maintain control over the self and to find the balance between breathing for energy and breathing for repose. Many of the voice exercises for vowels and consonants can be adapted as games: again, the sound and speech of many disabled people is distorted and needs additional help for clarity. As the range of voice develops, so does the expansion of role and character.

Day three:

Theory

(1) Assessment:

- (a) The use of checklists (see Appendix 1) in order to establish starting points for play.
- (b) Be aware of the complementarity between the Sherborne, Courtney, McClintock and Jennings assessment charts. All of them can be useful in different ways.

(2) The transition from everyday reality to the 'let's pretend' of playing:

- (a) Whatever form of play we use it establishes its own reality, with rules, and this is different from everyday reality.
- (b) This is not the same as going from reality to fantasy; play may include fantasy work, but is more often the reality of the play.
- (c) Play and dramatic play lead into artistic experience, especially drama.

It should be noted that play and drama can say the things that cannot be said in any other way.

(3) Education and therapy:

- (a) Through education, I am 'led through' a set of experiences from which I learn things, whether they are facts or skills.
- (b) In therapy, I am experiencing the processes of play and drama in order to make sense of myself and the world.
- (c) If my own experiences are the only basis for creativity, then I would find the limitations of my own script. Therefore, within the greater story, I can find my own story.

Practical work

Projective and role work

The following is a sequence which leads through from very simple Plasticine/clay-work to a whole-group community exercise. It is described below in numbered sequence and it will be apparent to the reader that it can be broken down into smaller sequences if necessary.

(1)   In small groups, soften and shape Plasticine. If people sing or hum to themselves, it will stop them getting self-conscious about what they are making.

(2)   Sit back-to-back with a partner, eyes closed, and play the Plasticine making a 'something'.

(3)   Open eyes and share with partner – often the pairs will have made similar shapes.

(4)   Sit back-to-back again with eyes closed, and make a 'nothing'. This instruction produces quite curious results as people discover that they have actually made something.

(5)   In groups of four, create a story that incorporates the four Plasticine objects.

(6)   'Become' the Plasticine objects and enact the story (the transition from projective work to role work).

(7)   Present a one-minute story that you have developed in your group.

(8)   In the same groups, use all the Plasticine (non-verbally) to create an environment.

(9)   Share the experience verbally: is it *where* you thought; is it *what* you thought; is it possible to agree?

(10)   Create a society to live in this environment: what way of life do these people have; what stories do they tell?

(11)   How do all the different societies in the group relate to each other, e.g. do they visit each other; do they trade; do they celebrate together?

(12)   Using newspaper or large drawing paper, create the spaces in between the societies – whether it is forest, sea, fields, etc.

(13)   Improvise an ambassador going from each community to visit the other communities: do they take or receive gifts?

(14)   Create a journey-story that involves leaving your community and returning to it.

The content of the three days described above was a very concentrated learning experience of playtherapy together with some
basic theory. Some of the group members felt that exercises of
this kind could be too difficult for children with severe learning
disabilities. We agreed to assess the truth or otherwise of this with
a group of children who were due to arrive the following week.

Twenty-five children with a range of disabilities arrived for the
playtherapy workshops. They were aged from six and upwards
with a wide range of ability and also some behaviour problems.
Several of the children were autistic and there were some mild
physical disabilities.

Day one

The adults and children form two large circles and from there
create small mixed groups. We start with an energetic warm-up
and then play animal rides to develop children's choices and trust.

Embodiment 1

(a) Floor-work – rolling, sliding, wheelbarrow.
(b) Sit one behind the other and move across the room without
     losing anybody.
(c) Develop the above into a story of a boat going fishing.
(d) Add a storm and storm movement. What happens to the boat
     and the fish?
(e) Sing together as you come home from the storm.
(f) All lean back-to-back and hum a song to relax and pause.
(g) The adults form a 'back' by going onto hands and knees side-
     by-side with other – children take it in turns to be gently
     rocked on the back (they can choose to lie on their back or
     front).
(h) Let the rocking become more risky as the movement becomes
     more vigorous.
(i) Let the back become a tunnel for the children to crawl
     through.
(j) All the adults stand up in one long row and form a tunnel for
     the children to crawl through their legs.

(*Note*: The tunnel exercise is enjoyed by all the children who are
racing round to try and go through it a second time. One older

boy, with severe learning disability and physical impairment, slowly plods through the entire tunnel, despite the disbelief of his teachers.)

(k)   Go back to the small groups and introduce the community that was established the previous week and create the dance and song of the tribe who inhabit this community.

Day two

Embodiment 2

(a)   Warm-up, using the 'Hokey-Kokey' for learning body-parts.
(b)   Use movement and song to learn people's names.
(c)   The rain-maker exercise (further development of the elements begun on day one with a storm).
(d)   The body-parts song which names and identifies different parts of the body.
(e)   Another body-parts song which both counts the body-parts and gives them sensations (e.g. 'Ten Little Fingers Dancing in a Row').
(f)   The adults stand opposite each other and join hands. A child lies face down with arms outstretched across the adults' arms. The adults are able to give the children a sense of flying by running with them across the room.
(g)   Similarly, a child can be rocked by adults using the same position; most children choose to lie on their backs for this exercise.
(h)   The whole group of adults then join hands, as above, and toss the child from one end of the line to the other: this was a high-risk game which even the most withdrawn children wanted to try.

Projection

(a)   Use the squiggle game – each person makes a mark on a piece of paper and slowly it turns into a picture that can be discussed.
(b)   Draw faces: some happy, some sad.

The day finishes with a relaxation exercise.

Day three

This is our last day of working with the children and it is important to consolidate the learning that has taken place with both them and the staff and to also give the staff a chance to develop some work of their own with the children.

Embodiment

(a)   Warm-up with name games.
(b)   Balancing and trust – head over heels and rides.
(c)   Recap yesterday's body-part songs.
(d)   Recap the pushing and pulling of the rolling.

Projection

(a)   Draw a person who looks happy, sad, angry (we use these pictures to develop facial expressions in children. Those who are unable to draw, join in the facial expression).
(b)   Create a face with the Plasticine and develop a group story.

CASE HISTORIES

The following are some examples of the staff's original work with the children together with reactions and observations:

'L is a child of nine years who has autistic tendencies. She took time to develop trust with her partner, but, by the third day, allowed herself to leave her head on the floor in the wheelbarrow exercise, to go head over heels, to pass through the tunnel, and to be rocked on her back. She found it difficult to resist being rolled. She created a face with two eyes. She established a good relationship with her partner and expressed sadness when her partner cried'.

'P is a mildly-retarded girl of twelve years. Although she is hyperactive and lacks eye contact, there was an improvement on this over the three days. Her concentration is poor, yet she learned the names of six people in two days. Although she could take risks in the tunnel and while being rocked, she was scared of the storm movement. She enjoyed the flying exercise and began to innovate in the play. She created a full face in Plasticine with all minor details. P initially could only talk about noodles which we had had for lunch that day. She called them worms and I was "the lady who eats worms"! She created a Plasticine face that was happy and said, "she's happy because her husband's died". The helper asked why she was happy since her husband had died and P replied, "He was a drinker and he used to beat her". She then created a story about two men and a bad snake. The bad snake came to bite them and a good snake made them better. Then a tree fell on them and she took on the role of a doctor who came to give the men injections and also gave one to the tree." '

'S is 15 years old and his head is heavy. He slouches on one side and appears to be in pain. He participated more because he was asked to than because he was necessarily enjoying what he was doing. In his drawing he was preoccupied with his friend who had been beaten up and felt good when he came crying to him. In-role, he refused to act an angry part and kept saying "can't do it." He was much more relaxed in group activities rather than in one-to-one work, especially since I was a woman.'

'K felt lost in the new environment because he was separated from his peer group. He did not respond freely to the trainee and was easily distracted by others. He did not like being contained because he was very stiff and tense in his body and initially did not develop any trust in the trainee; however, by the third session he opened up and seemed more relaxed and trusted the trainee. He participated in all the activities. He is observant, but observes when something takes his interest. He has a moderate memory and could recapitulate some of the activities on the last day. He did not have any interaction, either verbally or physically, with his peers or the adults, but by the third session he had started to communicate with the trainees as well as playing hide and seek with the other children in the community story.'

'U was very shy the first day he joined us. He refused to select an animal to sit on, but did not protest when helped onto one. He was quite overwhelmed initially and looked passive and uninterested. He found it difficult to make eye-contact with the trainer and was generally distracted by the group or the lights in the room. He did not want to speak and we had to find out his name from his teacher. The embodiment exercises like rolling and dragging on the floor interested him; however, he could not relax completely. His movement was not free–flowing. U had begun to relax by the end of the first day. He allowed himself to be contained without resistance. His eye-contact also improved with time. He spoke a few words which were not very clear. He gradually became more assertive and said "no" when he did not want to do something. U's projective skills are not well developed yet. He could hold a crayon and enjoyed scribbling on paper, but could not project any meaning through them. He played with Plasticine but could not name his creations. U could easily take on the role of a fish or a bird and found that very exciting. U is a slight and quiet child who probably needs his own time to build trust and open out into a delightful and bright child.'

'R shows very little mental retardation. Her chronological age is 13 years and she functions close to that level, although she is moody. She is well aware of the various parts of the body and has a reasonably good memory. This can be judged from the fact that she could identify the body-parts and also remember the related song. She established eye-contact at the beginning of the activities on day one and continued to be involved in all the activities until the end. R displayed sound projection capabilities. With the Plasticine she created an elephant which fitted well into the story spun by her group. Furthermore, the fact that she could construct a complete story with the squiggle picture amply demonstrated her imagination and sense of the whole. During the activities, it was observed that she was very self-conscious and uncomfortable while working with members of the opposite sex. This can probably be attributed to her conservative, rural family background. More work in projection and role activities would further benefit R.'

'B is 28 years old, has a short stature and a pronounced squint. He has fairly good comprehension, was co-operative, and could express himself in phrases. In the beginning he was shy and avoided eye-contact. His body movements were controlled and lacked spontaneity. He could not direct his strength to offer body-resistance. He was aware of his middle, and allowed others to contain him. Although he had the concept of his body-parts, during projective activities he could not align the facial parts correctly. He found playing with Plasticine appealing and he created objects from nature and the environment, but he lacked the imagination to relate the various objects to each other. When given a crayon, he began by drawing a faint dot in the corner and was gradually encouraged to fill the entire page. In role-play, he was able to mimic and innovate at times, but could not initiate imaginative play.'

'Amongst all the children, A has the maximum level of retardation; yet he is a very lovable and calm child. He worked with us for two days only as in the third session he was sick so he missed it. In the embodiment stage he initially needed support; free-flow movement was not there and he did not let his partner take his weight fully. After the containment exercises he built a contact with his partner and his body showed the signs of relaxation. He generally sits with his head downwards and avoids direct eye-contact. He is aware of his body-parts, but cannot indicate them with his hands. His spatial awareness is very weak. During projection exercises he was unable to play the squiggle game, but was totally involved and concentrated on scribbling the crayons on the paper. With encouragement and attention, we feel he can improve a lot, as within these two days we could notice distinct signs of improvement in him.'

'When all the students (trainee therapists) entered it seemed overwhelming not only for the children but for us as well. Giving them the choice of which adult they wanted to work with helped them to be more relaxed. Through the embodiment exercises, each student and trainee slowly formed a rapport. It was noticeable that the initial interactions were on an individual level, but over the three days, the dynamics changed and the students responded in their own way through the EPR process. This was one of the major goals achieved by this group. Throughout the embodiment stage, the students were initially hesitant when doing an activity on their own, but when it was demonstrated by the trainee they were willing to do it and to join in. As trainees, we had some discomfort because two of the students were adolescent boys; however, on days two and three the trainees were more comfortable with them. We moved from embodiment to projection and the drawing of a face. One of the students could not readily express his feelings or thoughts on an individual level: he found it easier when another student helped him. This was an encouraging sign that the students could help each other and not just rely on the trainees. On the third day the group process had reached a great level of communication between all members of the group. The trainees related not only to their own students but to other students in the group and vice versa. In the role stage, one of the students became very disturbed in the community exercise, but other group members helped him to be part of the play. One of the most noticeable features was that they helped another disabled person within the play – "The blind old man". This was a major theme which emerged within the group.'

The above programme shows what is possible in a very concentrated period of time with a group of children and adolescents with severe learning disability. It is clear from the above examples that even the most diffident children were able to improve their range of response; their memory and concentration, and their relationships. There was some interesting spontaneous creativity; for example, when one of the fishing boats went out to sea and threw out a fishing-line, one girl pretended to be caught on the fishing-line and to be hauled into the boat.

What is vital is that the playtherapist/leader feels confident in these sorts of exercises and is willing to allow the child's experience to be valid rather than imposing a conventional answer.

SUMMARY

This chapter illustrates how play in all its forms is a necessary part of children's lives – especially those with severe learning disabilities. It charts a progression using some techniques described in other chapters as well as some specifically described for learning disabled groups. A staff training programme is described as well as its adaptation to a particular group of children.

NOTES

[1]   It has taken many years for public and professional attitudes to begin to change towards the arts and disabled people. The Royal Shakespeare Theatre in Stratford-upon-Avon now has an annual production by the group Kaleidoscope in their winter visitors' programme.

[2]   It can be disastrous to implement a 'drama for change' programme if the ground work has not been done. The long-term care staff are normally the backbone of institutions (even with the changes of hostels, day centres and so on) and can be the resource for establishing play and drama work at grass roots level.

[3]   This is an excellent example of the culture and art of the society being used as a basis for the play and the drama. The larger-than-life epic usually provides the great story within which we can all find our own story.

REFERENCES

Berry, C. (1975) *Your Voice and How to Use it Successfully*. London: Harrap.

Brudenell, P. (1986) *The Other Side of Profound Handicap*. London: Macmillan.

Courtney, R. (1981) 'Developmental Drama Check List' In *Drama in Therapy* (Eds R, Courtney & G. Schattner), pp 21–26. New York: Drama Book Specialists.

Heathcote, D. (1981) *Drama and the Mentally Handicapped in Arts Disabilities* (Ed. G. Lord). London: Macmillan.

Lord, G. (Ed.) (1981) *The Arts and Disabilities*. London: Macmillan.

Lord, G. (ed.) (1985) *The Arts and Disabled People: the Attenborough Report*. London: Bedford Square Press.

Jennings, S. (1973) *Remedial Drama*. London: A & C Black.

Jennings, S. (1986) *Creative Drama in Groupwork*. London: Winslow Press.

Levete, G. (1982) *No Handicap to Dance*. London: Souvenir Press.

McLintock, A. (1984) *Drama for Mentally Handicapped Children*. London: Souvenir Press.

Sherborne, V. (1975) 'Movement for Retarded and Disturbed Children'. In *Creative Therapy* (Ed. S. Jennings), pp 68–90. London: Kemble Press.

Sherborne, V. (1990) *Developmental Movement for Children*. Cambridge: Cambridge University Press.

Tomlinson, R. (1982) *Disability Theatre and Education*. London: Souvenir Press.

Chapter 7

Referral, Diagnosis and Assessment

'Inch-worm, Inch-worm, measuring the marigold
You and your arithmetic will probably go far.'
(Danny Kaye as Hans Christian Anderson)

'I'm a quiet little horse I am, and the thought of going into the wide
world breaks my heart.
(Adventures of the Little Wooden Horse)

In this chapter we will consider the thinking through that is necessary before practice in order for playtherapists to feel sufficiently
supported and guided on the one hand and to feel confident
enough for some risk taking on the other. In both this chapter and
the following one, we are really addressing the playtherapist's
ritual/risk factor.

The previous chapters have considered the various developmental
contexts for this work, looked at a wide range of methods and their
application. As has been said earlier, the Playtherapy Method is a
multi-model intervention which takes as its basis the dramatic
nature of both human beings and play activity. However we need
to consider the reality of its application and, what actually happens
when a child comes into the room – what do we open our mouths
and say if anything at all?

REFERRAL FOR PLAYTHERAPY

Referral for playtherapy can arise from a carefully assessed situation that involves the professional team from social services,
health, education and probation, or from a haphazard response to
'do something'. The result of this latter initiative takes the form

of the playtherapist being asked, 'would you just . . .' (see also Chapter 9). Regrettably, there are times when it is felt necessary to be *seen* to be doing something – especially in relation to children – rather than first to think through an appropriate plan of action. It is to be hoped that the implementation of the Children Act 1991 will influence less acceptable procedures and involve families as a whole and not just the damaged children from those families.

In the case of the use of the Playtherapy Method, it is important that appropriate assessment and referral be made. It also makes a measurable difference to the outcome of the therapy if the family has been involved as much as possible. The playtherapist is not a substitute parent for the child, even though the playtherapy itself may facilitate some re-parenting. It is important for the child who continues to live at home not to feel a divided parental loyalty. In fostering too, it is important for the natural parents to have a place in the child's world. Too often in the past, attempts have been made to make the child 'forget' and make a new start in a new home, with new adults and new possessions; yet, as we saw earlier, it is so often the old and worn toy that is the 'treasure'.

OUTLINING THE PLAYTHERAPY PROCESS

Once assessment is complete (a process carried out with the family if possible), it is important that any decisions are explained (usually more than once) to all those concerned. Parents and other family members need to have playtherapy explained to them as much as the child him- or herself does; families need to understand that the child's behaviour may well deteriorate in the initial stages. Parents need to be reassured that the confidentiality of the therapy need not threaten them – that much of what the child communicates is private (just as all people need privacy) – and that the child will tell them things when he or she is willing and ready. If this is not made clear, many parents (and teachers too) will cross-examine children about what they have done and said in the session – and it can then be ridiculed or criticized. Most parents feel very guilty about the fact that their child needs therapy and ask the question 'Where did I go wrong?' They may resent what they may regard as the miracles that happen within a short space of time or even sabotage the sessions by arriving late, or cancelling them or under-mining the playtherapist's relationship with the child in some other way.

It may be that during the time of the child's playtherapy support can also be arranged for the parents – and indeed other members of the family – and, where family therapy resources are available, sessions for the family as a whole. While fundamental change can be brought about by working with the whole family, this does not necessarily exclude work with an individual as well. There is not scope here to properly debate the theory and practice of family therapy – whether systemic or strategic – except to suggest that the family therapist's belief in work in the here-and-now with the family as a whole represents a major breakthrough in the assumptions we make about therapy. The family therapist does not focus on the presenting patient, that is the person labelled as having the problem, but with the family as a whole, seeing the family as an interlocking system which has become dysfunctional. As is often the case, one member of the family can take on the problems on behalf of the family as a whole.

Case history

As an example of how an untreated family can manifest its dysfunction through taking it in turns to be seriously ill, we can look at the Parkin family. This family claimed they were ordinary, traditional and law-abiding. Mr Parkin owned a small grocery and general store with a sub-post office on the outskirts of a small country town. Mrs Parkin ran the house and occasionally helped her husband; Margaret, Robert and Anne were born within two or three years of each other. The family came to the attention of the GP when Mrs Parkin took her daughter Anne to the surgery on several occasions because she was 'poorly', 'sickly' or 'not eating'. At the same time, her mother would say to the GP, 'of course, I was like that as a child – I did not eat – I was thin – I missed school a lot – I was ill. . . .'

Margaret left home as soon as possible, having been the 'hard worker' at school. She promptly joined the Women's Royal Army Corps and applied to work overseas; she visited home once or twice a year when she was on leave.

Anne continued to have time off from school as well as invalid foods, tonics and vitamins bought by her mother. This continued for several years – although teachers had suggested that Anne might be anorectic – until she disappeared one day and was found sitting on a park bench, looking withdrawn and possibly in a psychotic state. She was admitted to hospital and given anti-depressants and a brief period of psychotherapy before being discharged and recommended to attend a day centre. She found a home in a half-way hostel, attended the day centre for some months, and had regular check-ups because she and her mother were both convinced that she had an organic problem. However she did not wish to return to her family home and continued to live in the hostel for a couple of years. She was still unwell, and found increasing difficulty in dealing with the imposed rules of the hostel.

Meanwhile, the parents continued as before and their son Robert left school and started working in the shop and post office with his father. Of her own accord, Anne made a decision to leave the hostel and live in a bed-sit on her own. In less than a month, Robert had a psychotic break-down and was sectioned and admitted to hospital. The recommendation came that he should leave home and live in a half-way hostel (he was still on medication) which he refused to do and went back home again. In a matter of weeks his mother developed a stomach ulcer which allegedly did not respond to treatment. Thus the role of 'patient' moved from daughter to son to mother. Meanwhile the family refused any type of intervention, believing that the only problems were physical ones. Robert still behaves strangely from time to time, something which usually precipitates a deterioration of Mrs Parkin's condition. Neither parent has any intention of encouraging Robert to leave home and sees it as his right to stay with them if he so chooses. The sisters Margaret and Anne survive by staying right away from the family.

Teaching point

The above example is an obvious illustration of a family which maintains its dysfunction by not allowing any disruption of the status quo. Although we might use psychoanalytic theory to offer explanations in the case of this family – as, for example, the unresolved Oedipal conflicts of Robert – we would be impelled to suggest that all the family members would need therapy of some kind. Notice how the father is strangely absent in the above scenario. In reality he *is* absent to his family because he is always busy checking stock and adding up figures and never around to be talked to or with. If the family were motivated to come for therapy then it would seem that here-and-now intervention with a systemic family therapist might well allow change.

In the above hypothesis, however, the family has to be both motivated and willing for change to take place. Very often therapists have to work with a child in need, without the co-operation

or more extended involvement of the family. Playtherapy intervention with the whole family is discussed later in this chapter.

DIAGNOSIS THROUGH PLAYTHERAPY?

It is often hoped that playtherapy will yield information that can be
used to diagnose the various problems that children manifest.
Some agencies see the function of playtherapy as being that very
thing – diagnostic and disclosure work. This comes about from
various needs, the obvious one of course being that for evidence
that will stand up in a court of law, and many child abuse cases
have not proceeded because children have been unable to testify
especially when they have had to face the perpetrator in an open
court.

Although currently there appears to be a change in the way such
cases are conducted, nevertheless there is still a preoccupation
with facts. The child is seen as a locked box and the therapist is
expected to find the key. As explained in Chapter 8, the roles in
terms of disclosure and therapy *must* be separated if there is to be
satisfactory healing intervention.

Furthermore, if a child appears grossly disturbed or damaged,
then diagnostic interviews and assessment are necessary if the
most appropriate form of therapy is to take place. This takes place
before the playtherapy or other intervention commences.

Usually a child psychologist and/or psychiatrist is involved in the
primary diagnostic period (together with reports from others who
have been involved such as social workers and teachers). Clinicians
state that formal diagnosis of childhood disorder should rely on
standardized, reliable clinical criteria. There are a number of standard tests which the reader may refer to in psychology texts. These
texts usually classify childhood disorders under the following
headings: developmental; behavioural; emotional; habit; learning
difficulties. Of course not all theorists agree what should come
under each of the headings (for example is anorexia nervosa classi-
fied as an emotional problem or a faulty habit?) and therefore the
best method of intervention!

It is not within the scope of this book to enter the debate which
surrounds many of these issues – not least the nature/nurture and
the behavioural therapy/psychodynamic therapy perennial – some
of them are illustrated in Chapter 1. We need to acknowledge that
playtherapists may have an orientation within only one model

(such as object relations or behaviouristic for example) or a variety of models (often termed the eclectic or multi-model) in relation to clinical theory. We shall discuss in the Chapter 9 the training of the playtherapist and the necessary basic clinical knowledge.

However the question that concerns us here is whether playtherapy methods can be used for diagnosis.

Behar and Rapaport (1983) say that play observation may be a useful *adjunct* in some circumstances, such as when:

(1)   contradictions or doubtful assertions are found in the reports of parents and teachers.
(2)   a discrepancy is sensed between reports and clinical observation.
(3)   the child is too young mentally to be interviewed verbally or when for a variety of reasons the verbal communications are suspect.
(4)   the child is too shy or too withdrawn to be otherwise engaged.

However, they also refer to 'the clinical, intuitive, hypothesis generating process which play interview provides.' This is similar to what Peter Brook calls 'the formless hunch' (Brook, 1988). Clinician and theatre artist alike are prepared to acknowledge that there is a non-quantifiable area of human observation based on 'gut reaction'.

Gut reaction plays a large part in the way we both assess and practise as artistic therapists of various kinds, especially in playtherapy when we may be working with children who are pre-verbal or non-verbal.

This intuitive 'hunch' may well be an indicator for therapeutic exploration but must not be confused with the therapist's interpretations and explanations of the child's play. However I would suggest that the 'hunch' is likely to be of use in the early playtherapy sessions when determining which direction to go (see the case histories of Penny and Shaun in the following Chapter for example); in diagnostic work interviews the intuitive impressions contribute to the overall picture.

In the next section we shall look at the several playtherapy assessment sessions that are usually necessary before a programme can begin.

PLAYTHERAPY ASSESSMENT

When a child has been referred for playtherapy, it is necessary first to have several playtherapy assessment sessions. These enable the therapist *and* the child to 'take stock'. Decisions need to be made about the optimum number of sessions (3 or 4?; over a period of 6 weeks?; over 3, 6, 9, 12 months?; how often? weekly? fortnightly?). The following are some questions that need to be asked during the first and second sessions:

- What does the child want from the therapy?
- What does the therapist want from the therapy?
- Does the child actually understand what playtherapy is?
- What materials in the playtherapy room draw the child?
- Where does the child respond on the embodiment-projection-role (EPR) paradigm?
- How does the child respond on the ritual/risk (R/R) scale?

Many people may feel, like Oaklander and others, that the therapist can start from where the child is and then see what happens.

'My goal is to help the child become aware of herself and her existence in her world.'

and

'The process I present is self-monitoring, I believe there is no way you can make a mistake if you have good will and refrain from interpretation and judgements – if you accept the child with respect and regard.'

and

'I never force a child to do or say something he absolutely does not want to do or say. I try to avoid interpretations, so I check out my own guesses and hunches with the child. If he's not interested in responding, that's fine. I don't insist that he 'own' anything if he needs to keep things safely protected.'

Violet Oaklander *Windows to Our Children*, 1978

Virginia Axline puts forward her non-directive approach:

'Non-directive play therapy, as we have said before may be described as an opportunity that is offered to the child to experience growth under the most favorable conditions. Since play is his natural medium for self-expression, the child is given the opportunity to play out his accumulated feelings of tension, frustration, insecurity, aggression, fear, bewilderment, confusion.'

and

'Because primary emphasis is placed upon the active participation of the self in this growth experience, the term non-directive seems inadequate. While this term does accurately describe the role of the counsellor, in that he maintains sufficient self-discipline to restrain any impulses which he might have to take over the client's responsibility, it is certainly inaccurate when applied to the role of the client. Instead, self-directive therapy seems to be a more accurate and more honestly descriptive term.'

Virginia Axline *Play Therapy*, 1947; 1983

Margaret Lowenfeld (1935) goes as far as to state that the true observation of children at play is impossible because it means the presence of an adult. At her Institute of Child Psychology, an out-patient clinic for the treatment and study of children, she conducted a programme twice weekly for children with a variety of problems including: emotional disturbance; chronic disorders such as epilepsy asthma, catarrh, debility, constipation, enuresis; children who were unable to adjust themselves socially; and children with educational difficulties. An intelligence test was given by a worker with whom the child was unfamiliar, to every child before its entry to the playroom.

Lowenfeld was very strict about the playrooms being only for the children and the therapists – parents were not allowed in; and therapists had to work at the same physical level as the child. However she was also concerned that the therapist's scale of *values* is different from the scale of values of the child – and that the difference is so radical that the adult can only be experienced as judgemental or criticizing.

Sara Smilansky (1968) identified six evaluating factors in relation to sociodramatic play. She makes use of these in observation of children's play both before and after play intervention to test whether change has taken place:

(1)   Imitative role-play – the child undertakes a make believe role and expresses it in imitative action and/or verbalisation.
(2)   Make-believe in regard to objects – movements or verbal declarations are substituted for real objects.
(3)   Make-believe in regard to actions and situations – verbal descriptions are substituted for actions and situations.
(4)   Persistence – the child persists in a play episode for at least ten minutes.
(5)   Interaction – there are at least 2 players interacting in the framework of the play episode.

(6) Verbal communication – there is some verbal interaction related to the play episode.

These categories are very useful in a diagnostic period[1] when considering which direction the playtherapy needs to go. However the above categories fall under the third stage of EPR since they start with the capacity to role play. Therefore they would be more useful for the Playtherapy Method as part of a wider conceptual framework.

Smilansky emphasises the difference between sociodramatic play (or social dramatic play) and play with rules, and suggests that they are two separate psychological systems. According to her observations, children may engage in play with rules and be unable to participate in sociodramatic play.

Eleanor Irwin (1983) describes how she uses dramatic play materials to stimulate fantasy and play in several methods in diagnosis and treatment. She says:

'Each offers an opportunity to observe the child's verbal and non-verbal responses; the thinking and decision making process; the response to and the use of materials; the process, form, and content of the play; and the child's interaction with the therapist.'

and

'Experience has indicated that a variety of diagnostic approaches are helpful, as each gives data about different aspects of personality functioning. In addition, variety allows for the child's idiosyncratic responses to materials and media and gives the adult a chance to learn about natural interests and experiences.'

The several play therapy orientations described above, all emphasize the importance of play in diagnosis and assessment but demonstrate a very wide spectrum of approaches, which range from 'the way in and follow the child' to the more 'interpretive and psychoanalytic view'.

EMBODIMENT PROJECTION AND ROLE IN DIAGNOSIS AND ASSESSMENT

In the previous chapters, EPR as a developmental way of working is described with a variety of methods for application in the play-

therapy setting both with children and adolescents. Having described the component parts of each of the stages and the broad
ages at which they will occur, we are now in a position to consider
EPR in relation to diagnosis and assessment.

We must remember that any chart or form for recording our
work is as good as the categories on the chart and I would re-
commend playtherapists to evolve and experiment with their own
charts.

Figure 7.1 is an example of an EPR recording sheet that I am
developing at the moment. It has been given to a large number of
people to use who will then make suggestions as to modifications.

Under each of the developmental headings is a list of appropriate categories against which the playtherapist records the child's
responses – whether something has been engaged with, avoided or
no response. Note that this is not a recording sheet for content of
the sessions as described later in Chapter 8.

When using EPR in diagnosis it is particularly important for the
therapist to have an overarching frame, a total structure within
which to work, because EPR includes a wide spectrum of media
and materials. Within this framework the therapist follows the
child during any one session. Some playtherapy methods in themselves impose a structure because of the range of methods and
materials.

In the above example of observations of Jane, we can see that in
the first session there was no embodiment apart from at the very
end when she held the therapist's hand as she left the room; she
did not use the room spatially apart from sitting at the table. Under
projection she avoided sand/sand and water and clay/Plasticine
and used crayons to draw the rose bush. (see Oaklander 1978).
Under role any movement and gesture was avoided but she joined
in with nursery rhymes.

By session 2 she holds the therapist's hand on arrival and claps
hands in a hand clapping song. She moves between the table and
the cushion (embodiment). She again avoids the sand and water
but briefly engages with the Plasticine and crayons and draws a
house and garden (projection). She sings nursery rhymes again
very quietly (role).

In session 3 there is brief eye contact and the dolls' house is
included in her spatial orientation (embodiment). She takes water
for the dolls' house bath. She moves the dolls' house toys around.
Then draws a garden with a baby in a pram (projection). She sings
and hums to herself and sustains a sequence of events through

EMBODIMENT-PROJECTION-ROLE OBSERVATION

Name: Jane   Dramatherapist/Playtherapist: SJ

dob 8.1.84   aged 7 years

		Session 1	2	3	Recommendations
	Date:	3.4.91	10.4.91	17.4.91	
EMBODIMENT:					
1.	Touch. Eye-contact	held hand on leaving	held hand on arrival	brief eye contact	E needs
2.	Spatial Awareness	sat at table	sat at table/cushion	moved to dolls hse	to be
3.	Working With/Against	—	—	—	developed
4.	Whole Body	—	—	—	slowly as
5.	Body Parts		hand clapping + singing →	D	she gains
6.	Body Self/Image				confidence
7.	Mimicry/Innovation		mimicry	innovated dolls house	
8.	Other				
PROJECTION:					
1.	Sand/Sand & Water	avoided →	D	water for dolls house bath	Well engaged with P
2.	Clay/Plasticine	—	rolled in ball	—	obvious starting
3.	Pencil/Crayons	✓	✓	✓	point with
4.	Paint (finger/brush)	—	—		1) plasticine
5.	Single Image/Whole Picture	rosebush	house and garden	garden with baby in pram	2) drawing 3) dolls
6.	Single/Large Toys	—	—	dolls house toys	house
7.	Environmental *	—			
8.	Other				
ROLE					
1.	Body Movement/Gesture	avoided	clapped hands	singing & moving	Role work
2.	Sound/Speech	sung nursery rhymes	sang to self	Quietly	through
3.	Mimicry/Innovation	mimicry	innovation	innovation	dolls
4.	Brief/Sustained	sustained	both	sustained	
5.	Relationship with another role			[with dolls]	No role
6.	Role Development				play until
7.	Development Scene/Situation				E is
8.	Other				addressed

GENERAL OBSERVATIONS

Jane is a v. withdrawn child - no eye contact until 3rd session; v. engaged with rose-bush + dolls house - more time needed - reassurance? Family support?

* houses/jungles, etc., with boxes and material

Fig. 7.1 An EPR recording sheet.

the dolls' house dolls (role). She has started to develop role but through the medium of the toys.

Based on these three early sessions the therapist has a guide line of *how* to work with the child and will have noted the lack of embodiment work so crucial for later growth and maturation. Look at the recommendations on this chart. Why might the therapist have made these recommendations? This child is very withdrawn physically and makes no contact or attempts to initiate contact; the indicator is that the child is prepared to play safely through the medium of the dolls' house. Role-play at this stage would be contra-indicated until some inner strengths and trust had been built up through embodiment. Therefore the chart gives a diagnostic indicator of the areas to develop with the child.

RITUAL/RISK OBSERVATION

Let us also look at Jane in relation to ritual and risk (Fig. 7.2). The ritual/risk paradigm has been developed, again, as a broad diagnostic and assessment tool to enable the therapist to look at the balance of content in any one session.

Under ritual we consider known, safe and repetitive dramatic rituals that the child has already established; such as a clapping song, jumping game or dance (embodiment); an arrangement of toys or the dolls' house or a picture that is repeated each time (projection); or the same scene, story or song and actions (role).

The chart in Figure 7.3 is divided into ritual/risk in relation to spatial awareness and use of media.

In session 1 the therapist has suggested that there was no risk at all but the known factor of sitting at the table. However, she later suggests that maybe coming into the room itself was a risk! In the use of media there was minimal risk in the drawing of the rose bush. The singing of nursery rhymes would come under ritual.

In session 2 there is an increase in taking spatial risk because Jane moves between the table and the cushion and a sharp increase in use of media with new pictures and Plasticine.

In session 3 both areas of risk have increased – the use of media substantially more than of space. However this is also an indicator for the pacing of the intervention. Because the child has noticeably increased the risk factor in just three sessions in relation to media, it is recommended that role work is not attempted with the child until there is more embodiment.

RITUAL-RISK OBSERVATION

Name: Jane   Dramatherapist/Playtherapist: SJ

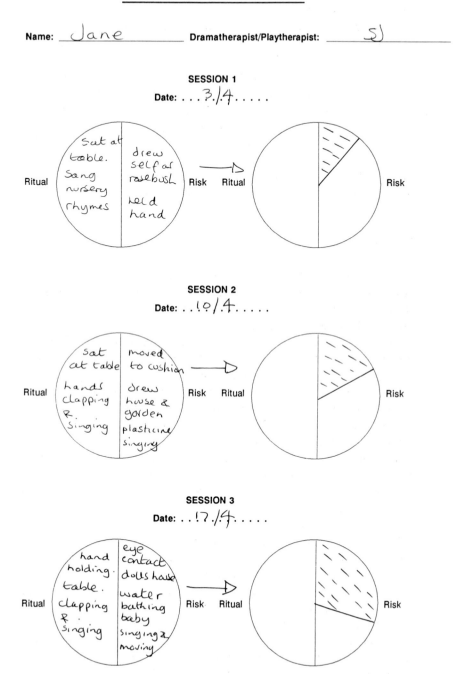

SESSION 1
Date: ...3./.4.....

Ritual: Sat at table. Sang nursery rhymes | drew self as rosebush. held hand : Risk

SESSION 2
Date: ..10/.4.....

Ritual: Sat at table hands clapping & singing | moved to cushion. drew house & garden plasticine singing : Risk

SESSION 3
Date: ..17./.4.....

Ritual: hand holding. table. clapping & singing | eye contact dolls house water bathing baby singing & moving : Risk

Fig. 7.2 Ritual/risk observation.

RITUAL-RISK OBSERVATION

Name: _Jane_   **Dramatherapist/Playtherapist:** _SJ_

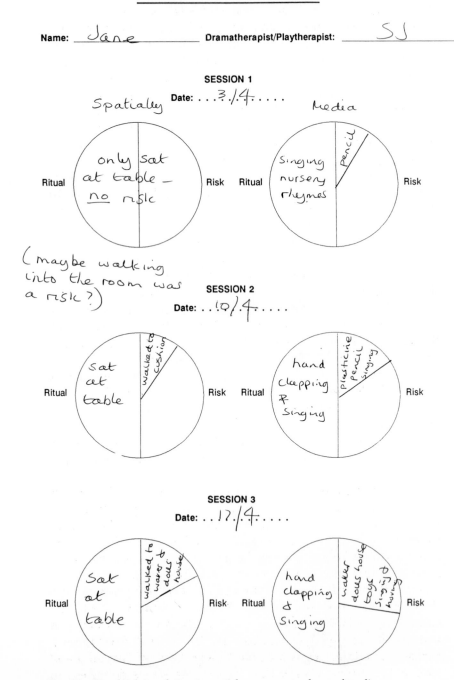

SESSION 1

Date: ...3./.4......

Spatially   Media

Ritual — only sat at table — no risk — Risk   Ritual — Singing nursery rhymes / Pencil — Risk

(maybe walking into the room was a risk?)

SESSION 2

Date: ...10/.4......

Ritual — Sat at table / walked to cushion — Risk   Ritual — hand clapping & singing / Plasticine Pencil singing — Risk

SESSION 3

Date: ...17./.4......

Ritual — Sat at table / walked to wave to dolls house — Risk   Ritual — hand clapping & singing / water dolls house toys singing noises — Risk

Fig. 7.3 Ritual/risk in relation to spatial awareness and use of media.

In the use of the ritual/risk paradigm, again, we are looking at the balance between these two ingredients, especially in such a potentially volatile area as dramatic playtherapy. Generally speaking the more disturbed the child, the less risk is needed in the early stages and a greater emphasis on ritual and the building up of security is necessary. This covers the whole range of disturbed behaviours including those children who exhibit stereotyped movements and sounds (often mis-named rituals). The child who persistently rocks for example has established a pattern to ward off the unexpected or disturbing. A therapist needs to start working with this pattern rather than presenting alternative media.

The child who is physically grounded, who responds well on the embodiment work and has a existing balance of ritual/risk is usually ready to develop innovatory risk work as well as consolidating it through ritual.

I want to mention here the very useful chart in the Veronica Sherborne book (1990) which has been previously mentioned. The chart may be used by people who buy the book for the recording of their work and it gives many of the basic categories that we are looking for in embodiment work, including the child's awareness of the whole body and body parts and the child's relationship with the partner and with peers. This form is an ideal one to use in combination with the EPR and the risk/ritual forms.

There are other useful observation charts for early dramatic play work with children including Richard Courtneys check list (see appendix), and Barbara Sandberg's Developmental check list for Drama, in Schattner and Courtney (1981). Although designed for children with severe learning disability, there is also a useful check list in Anne McClintock, Drama for Mentally Handicapped Children.

You may of course want to develop your own checklist which suits your particular way of working. Study the charts that other people have formulated and how they apply and their short-comings. Then make sure you have a broad understanding of child observation – there are many books on this subject. However, remember that even the books on child observation will have an orientation from the writer. For example, there are books on psychoanalytic child observation that follow Kleinian or more broad-based object-relations theories; there are books on play activities that can be observed at various ages in 'normal' development. Perhaps now is the right moment to refer back to Chapter 1 and look at the various clinical theories and age stages described. In relation to the Playtherapy Method within the broad frame of clinical understanding, remember that we are looking at the dramatic development of the child.

The dramatic development of children through their life journeys of dramatic stages demonstrate that as human beings we are artistic and aesthetic and that these qualities are necessary for survival.

By describing human beings as having dramatic personas, I am not referring to the roles we play in our day-to-day discourse. I am referring to the dramatic reality – the playful reality where our symbolic imagination can pretend and hypothesize.

BASIC PH AND 6PSM AS METHODS OF ASSESSMENT

Mooli Lahad has evolved, in his clinical work with Israeli children under stress, a statistically viable method of assessment before therapeutic intervention is undertaken. He is primarily interested here in the notion of children who are stressed, as well as children who are described as having a problem, and his analysis is a multi-model one which considers the coping mechanisms that each child already has. Lahad's work is an ideal method to combine with EPR and risk/ritual observation because it assists us to vary the therapy to fit the child rather than fitting a child into a particular framework or reference.

> BASIC Ph is a model for understanding, coping and resilience.
> 'Stressful situations become unbearable when they are prolonged and we are no longer capable, using the resources at our disposal, to be rid of or to lessen the stress. Under circumstances where repeated attempts do not avail, the situation could turn into a crisis. Many times a situation becomes a crisis because the individual uses 'more of the same thing' to be rid of the stress: in other words, a person becomes set in the mould, using the same mode of coping endlessly, neither progressing nor changing anything. In this case the crisis stems from being stuck or from inflexibility. On a primary prevention level, my 'multi-modal approach' aims to teach the individual a number of different options in order to gain flexibility in coping with stressful situations, rather than reaching a dead-end.'
>
> (Lahad, 1992)

Lahad rates the child on the six point scale of:

Belief   Social   Cognition
Affect   Imagination   Physical

i.e. BASIC Ph. (see Fig. 7.4).

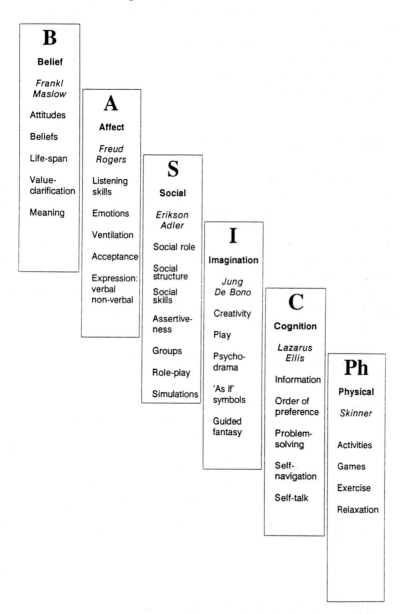

Fig. 7.4 C. Lahad 1992 (reproduced with permission).

He does this through six-part story making (6PSM) which is drawn by the child. It has the following elements in it:

(1)   Main character – hero or heroine.
(2)   Task or mission of the main character.
(3)   Who or what helps the main character?
(4)   Who or what obstacle prevents the accomplishment of the task?
(5)   How will the main character cope with the obstacle?
(6)   Then what happens?

Lahad says that the therapist listens on several levels: the tone in which the story is told after it has been drawn; the context of the story and its message (themes and I would add the sub-text); and the dominant coping modes of the story (BASIC Ph).

Through this approach in assessment together with the Play-therapy Method one is able as far as possible to both understand the drama the child needs to perform as well as the witnessing role that they need from the therapist.

EPR, ritual/risk, BASIC Ph and 6PSM are all methods that help the therapist to discover where a child is ready to start and where the strengths and weaknesses are in relation to the creative act – whether body work, projective play, enactment or story making. Such assessment enables us to take a broad view of the child in the here-and-now and give pointers as to the most valuable starting point or range of techniques for therapeutic intervention.

SUMMARY

This chapter has been concerned with the way we approach children in relation to diagnosis and assessment. It has looked at several approaches and described in some detail EPR, ritual/risk, BASIC Ph and 6PSM. EPR and ritual/risk are concerned with the broad categories of dramatic material that the child relates to. Whereas BASIC Ph and 6PSM assesses the resilience and coping skills of the child before intervention takes place.

REFERENCES

Axline, V. (1947; 1969) *Play Therapy*, p 16. New York: Ballantine.
Behar, D. & Rapaport, J.L. (1983) 'Play Observation and Psychiatric Diag-

nosis'. In *Handbook of Playtherapy* (Eds. C.E. Schaefer & K. O'Connor), p 197. New York: John Wiley.

Brook, P. (1988) *The Shifting Point*. London: Methuen.

Courtney, R. & Schattner, G. (1981) *Drama in Therapy. Volume 1. Children*. New York, Drama Book Specialists.

Irwin, E. (1983) 'The Diagnostic and Therapeutic Use of Pretend Play'. In *Handbook of Playtherapy* (Eds. C.E. Schaefer & K. O'Connor), p 155. New York: John Wiley.

Lahad, M. (1992) 'Story Making in Assessment Methods for Coping with Stress: six-piece story-making and BASIC Ph'. In *Dramatherapy Theory and Practice 2* (Ed. S. Jennings), pp 150–163. London: Routledge.

Lowenfeld, M. (1935; 1991) *Play in Childhood*, p 27. London: MacKeith Press.

McClintock, A. (1984) *Drama for Mentally Handicapped Children*. London: Souvenir Press.

Oaklander, V. (1978) Windows to Our Children. Moab, Utah: Real People Press.

Smilansky, S. (1968) *The Effects of Sociodramatic Play on Disadvantaged Pre-School Children*. New York: John Wiley.

Chapter 8

Common Difficulties in Playtherapy Practice

'I have drunk and seen the spider.'

The Winter's Tale II, i

'Little Miss Muffet
Sat on a Tuffet
Eating her Curds and Whey
There came a Big Spider
And sat down beside Her
And Frightened Miss Muffet away'

Nursery Rhyme

'What, has this thing appear'd again tonight?'

Hamlet I, i[1]

It is all very well for people who specialize in work with children, such as myself, to describe this work with children and their families as if it all happens in an ideal way – stages undertaken in the appropriate order – techniques received enthusiastically – colleagues and families always co-operative – unlimited resources – and a well–equipped working area. Of course it is not like this at all and the playtherapist can become quite overwhelmed by the difficulties of actually starting practice. I try to address some of these issues in Chapters 9 and 10 as they relate to resources, the context of practice and the playtherapist's professional role and training.

The intention in this chapter is to develop the idea of the practical reality of the application of playtherapy. The hope is to assist the fledgling playtherapist to avoid some of the common pitfalls which make this work even more stressful than it already is.

AN APPROACH TO DIFFICULT SITUATIONS IN PRACTICE

This chapter looks at the more difficult situations that the play-therapist may have to face at any give time, including work with children who have been abused. There is a tendency for some people to develop specialisms within playtherapy especially in working with child sexual abuse. I would like to suggest here that the playtherapist needs to retain a spectrum of practice which includes both therapeutic play and preventative play in order to retain a balanced overview as well as the appropriate detachment.

The motivations of the playtherapist will be considered in more depth in the final chapter. It is worth repeating here, however, that if we choose to work with damaged children then we must be prepared to acknowledge our own internal damaged child, and seek personal therapy for ourselves. If we avoid this, then we are in danger of exploiting the child – of searching for our own resol-utions through our work with children.

STRUCTURING THE INTERVENTION

The following 12 progressions in 3 stages may help playtherapists to pace their intervention, to be able to get into a rhythm of playtherapy with the child or children. This then becomes the structure within which the child meets the therapist. The stages do not follow in a straight line and earlier stages are returned to and worked with in different ways. EPR will occur at each stage.

Pre session: The child is referred and clinical information (if appro-priate) is available.

Stage 1 (warm up)
(1) *Meeting the child*: establishing roles and relationships; es-tablishing the framework and ground rules (questions/ explanations, etc.).
(2) *Random play*: diagnostic/assessment sessions: use of EPR, risk/ritual observation, BASIC Ph, 6PSM.

(A lot of checking out during this time; further questions and testing by child).

Stage 2 (development: engagement and interaction)
(3) *Basic trust*: some risk taking with self and other; some sharing but also testing.

(4) *Basic interaction*: therapist figures more in the play; dramatic relationship is beginning.

Teaching point

It will be helpful if the playtherapist remembers that his or her relationship with the child is a dramatic one – that he or she is engaged through role and character for the duration of the dramatic play and may therefore be flexible according to the child's needs

---

(5) *Developed dramatic play*: awareness of sub-texts; greater risk taking.
(6) *Therapist as actor*: when the child delegates 'risky' roles.
(7) *Therapist as audience*: important for witnessing what the child needs to be witnessed.
(8) *Therapist as co-actor*: participates with the child's direction in the dramatic scene; deeper engagement.

Stage 3
(9) *Post-dramatic play*: therapist and child are able to reflect on the drama.
(10) *Re-working scenes*: the child is able to re-direct scenes and explore different outcomes.
(11) *Integration of experience*: the child can view the drama as a whole and recognise self in drama and drama in self.
(12) *Closure and lights up*: working toward the ending and walking away from the drama and the relationship.

It will be clear from the above that the child develops deeper engagement and interaction in the play and therefore deeper disclosure, usually at a symbolic level. It is here that the play-therapist must be especially vigilant and not change the frame of reference. If the child discloses within the play then any exploration must be done *within the play and not through the goalposts being moved* otherwise the child will become more insecure.

Before starting any playtherapy with a child, there must be some idea of duration – and remember that a child's memory has a limited span. Open-ended playtherapy can produce a lot of insecurity ending up with the child becoming grossly dependent. Usually the Playtherapy Method, because it mobilises many resources in the child from the beginning, is used for short- and medium-term therapy, though the method is perfectly appropriate if longer term work is necessary. I prefer to have a series of contracts negotiated with the child, which then can be reviewed if either therapist or child request it. For example, a period of 3 diagnostic sessions followed by a contract for 6 further sessions (stages 2 and 3) is a reasonable short term contract and one that the child can grasp. Further lengths of time can be negotiated as required, and if there are resources then a longer term contract, say 3 to 6 months, can follow. However if there is no more time available, the child must know that clearly at the outset.

I spoke above about the rhythm of playtherapy and this takes time for the newly trained therapist to tune into. Detailed recording of each session and the guidance of an experienced supervisor will assist this. Figure 8.1 is a sample recording sheet that can be used with an individual child.

You will notice how I have included on the recording sheet the therapist's reflections before the session. We have discussed 'gut feeling' earlier in this book and I want to emphasise the importance of the creativity of the playtherapist in relation to the client's play and drama. You will be left with a host of impressions after sessions and the temptation is to tie it all up in meaningful explanations.

Having recorded a session, and, we said, that takes at least as long as the session itself (and in the early stages probably longer), allow the material to 'free-float' from time to time – scan your own reactions and association to what went on in the session. A detailed example of that process can be found in Dramatherapy with Families, Groups and Individuals, Chapter Four, (Jennings 1990).

Every playtherapist will have several internal states that will assist when both processing material as well as practising it:

- the internal child   What sort of child is yours – 'good'? naughty? shy? creative? playful?
- the internal client   Have you understood your own internal client – pain and damage as well as joy?
- the internal therapist   The person who is professionally trained and acts as your guide and informs you how to work.
- the internal supervisor   A benign support, assists you when stuck, backs up or challenges judgement if you are ambivalent.

BRIEF RECORDING OF PLAYTHERAPY SESSION

Childs Name   Playtherapist
Session Number   Date

Therapists thoughts before session:

Possible media and themes:

Mood/atmosphere at beginning: child
                                   therapist

Description of actual media and methods used:

E
P
R

Description of content expressed through above:

Fig. 8.1   Recording sheet for a playtherapy session.

- the internal creative actor   Usually works well with the internal child – is a resource of ideas and creativity – especially when you are even more stuck!

All these internal states need addressing outside your playtherapy practice: personal therapy for your internal client; proper training for your internal therapist; and regular supervision as will be discussed in the following chapter. Your internal child and creative actor both need a lot of nourishment and stimulus away from the work setting, indeed for their own sake. Playtherapy should not be used to satisfy these aspects of yourself. If you believe in creative play, then you believe in it for yourself as well!

Graph of levels of engagement throughout the session

Mood/atmosphere at closure: child

                                  therapist

Thoughts on the session: the child
                              the dramatic play

                              the self

Any action which needs to be taken?

Thoughts for the next session:

WORKING WITH CHILD ABUSE

As more and more incidents of child abuse of all kinds are being reported – and tidal waves of accusation and counter-accusation are being made – the hapless child can become the victim of the system and not just of the abuse itself. It is not apposite here to discuss the full ramifications of the current child abuse controversy – that would require another book. However, it is ever more important in the current climate that the playtherapist feels equipped to work with abuse.

First, let us recall that it is not for the playtherapist to both diagnose *and* treat child abuse, whatever form of abuse is involved: physical, sexual or emotional. If the playtherapy is being used diagnostically then it will be part of a range of assessments that are made prior to treatment and the child needs to know that information gleaned is not necessarily confidential. The playtherapist will be part of the team and will not be the person presenting evidence in court – if court proceedings are involved. It should be noted that evidence from symbolic play on its own is not usually sufficient evidence for court cases.

Diagnostic techniques

I am not a playtherapist who advocates diagnostic work using anatomically explicit dolls; both play and reality converge in these dolls and the fact that children may play in sexually explicit ways is not necessarily a sign of sexual abuse. The child may well, through BASIC Ph or 6PSM, be able to communicate stories of their abuse, but as diagnostic assessment for *evidence*, this would need to be tested both in and out of the play reality.

When playtherapy is used for the treatment of the child, the focus is different. There is less pressure on 'disclosure work' and on testing whether or not we think something is *true*. We start from the premise that everything the child tells us is true – *at some level* – and it becomes apparent during the therapy which these levels are and how much needs to be explicit and how much can stay within the symbolism of the play.

> 'However damaged the child – one reason for the playtherapy is to assist the child discover healing metaphors to facilitate the process of repair.'
>
> (Lahad, 1992)

However distressing we may find the child's situation, the most important quality we can give the child is that of belief. It is appropriate that the child knows that we can feel sorrow, anger and pain through our empathy, (not our sympathy) – as long as it is the child's pain we are sharing and not superimposing our own.

Case history

Polly was referred for playtherapy at the age of twelve following increasing outbursts of anti-social behaviour after she started secondary school – truanting, stealing, violent temper episodes. The school had said she was disruptive and a trouble-maker, and made life difficult for teachers since she was a leader; nevertheless, she was well-liked and some teachers expressed genuine affection towards her although at the same time they found her impossible.

She presented for her first session as wiry, tough and self-sufficient – with no intention of allowing me near her. She needed a lot of assurance that I was not going to *make* her do anything: 'Just don't make me do anything – that's all – just don't make me . . .' and I would respond, 'so you choose something' and she would say 'nah, nothing!' This became our ritual game at the beginning of the session. Polly then went on to say could she just 'chat a bit' – and feeling reassured that it was all right, she spent her time telling me bits of life-history from the recent past and the present (can a life history be in the present?).

Teaching point

Polly's request to 'just chat' is her way of wanting to play – she is fully engaged; motivated to attend the sessions; is never late; but needs to do it in her own way and at her own pace.

Polly then said how important it was for her not to be weak – and that she must never be 'caught out' – meaning that others must never get the better of her. I introduced her to the technique of mapping in which one creates a 'map' of the particular time in one's life that is significant. Maps have signposts, roads, paths, stop-go, buildings and environments and Polly got into the habit of drawing a map when she was describing a particular time in her recent past. These drawings were symbolic – certainly, but also with a logic all of their own. She began to draw a map of where she had lived when she was six (see Figs 8.2 and 8.3). She drew the tower block of flats and said, 'and down this road leads to the police station – where it all happened.'

I knew the clinical account of her examination for abuse by a police doctor, but her description went like this:

'My Mum screamed and carried me into the flats and rang the police and said I had been attacked – and a car arrived sirens blazing – and my Mum said that a man on the playground had attacked me. They sent policemen to look for him and took us to the station – everything was in such a hurry and people were panicking – they made me lie on a bed – there were lots of bright lights and a doctor examined me – and these other people held me down because I was screaming.'

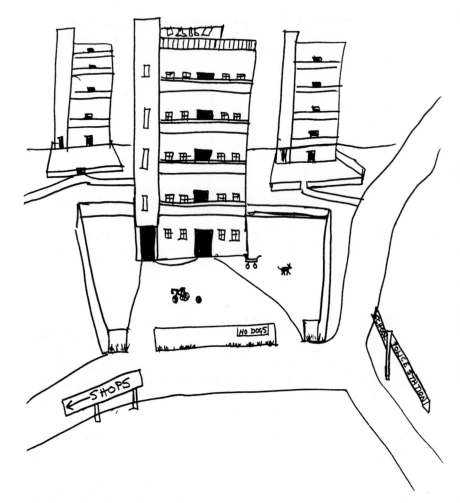

Fig. 8.2   Polly's outside map.

Polly has no memory of the alleged abuse – all her mother could tell her was that she had gone to the shops and she heard her scream – 'No, No, No' – her mother looked over the balcony and saw a man running away and her daughter crying. She ran down to fetch her and Polly said she had been told to do something naughty – so then her mother rang the police. However, as can be seen from the description above, she recalled the secondary abuse very clearly.

In a subsequent session, Polly was mapping where she had lived in more detail. She had regretted moving from that place since her mother wanted to take her away from where everything had happened, and she said: 'I *do* remember'. She promptly described how a boy (boy?) had come

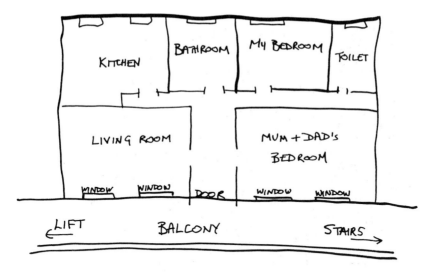

Fig. 8.3 Polly's inside map.

up to her and asked her to take down her knickers so he could have a look – she shouted 'NO' and he ran away – she started to cry and her mother came. Polly was certain it was a teenage boy who lived in the next street, although her mother was sure it was a man – the mother insisted that the family move away where nobody knew them in order to 'make a fresh start.' Polly was fetched from school one day to go to the new house and hadn't even been told they were moving.

Teaching point

It is important to note from the above case history how the secondary abuse of Polly's medical examination masked the first experience which seems to have been an indecent request rather than any sexual contact. Polly appears to have dealt with the situation by shouting 'NO' quite appropriately, when there had been a series of dramatic responses which all were experienced as abusive. The sudden move to the new house, loss of friends, and above all no explanation, culminated in making Polly feel that her only way forward was to be tough and in control.

It should be remembered that even when a child has been severely abused and this has necessitated the child being taken to a place of safety and the abuser being placed in custody, if a parent or sibling is involved, the child will need to work through many ambivalent feelings. However angry the child may feel, he or she also needs to express love and grief and the loss of people and places. Often the child is unable to express the anger since so many of his or her own feelings are confused in relation to the abuse (Cattanach, 1992), and many children blame themselves, especially when mothers have told daughters that it is their fault that their fathers abused them. The healing metaphor in the playtherapy needs to allow the child to express the multiple feelings towards the abuser and the abuse.

In her excellent book *Play Therapy with Abused Children*, Ann Cattanach describes very poignantly the way children feel when they have been abused. The children are able to articulate through the playtherapy such thoughts as, 'Don't do that to my granddaughter. The babies' grandad did it. Poor babes.' This illustrates how children can be articulate about their experiences through the medium of the playtherapy[2].

Case history

Shaun was referred for playtherapy at the age of eight, after he had been taken into care, because of incestuous abuse by an uncle. He was awaiting a long-term foster family. He was staying in a children's home with a large number of 'mixed' children who were variously 'in transit'. Shaun had precipitated a referral for therapy by persistently scarring himself on his arms with sharp metal objects. His psychiatric assessment had shown no severe mental health 'problem' and the observation was that this was a child who was still in shock.

At the first session Shaun sat mute, twiddling with a button and occasionally picking up something and putting it down in a desultory way. He rarely looked at the playtherapist but gazed towards the window and the door.

Teaching point

The playtherapist is having to select which area of this plethora of experience might be helpful for Shaun – especially as he is not yet in a permanent place of safety. Note how she presents that selection to the child, an intuitive hunch that seems to pay off.

THERAPIST: Shaun, it is your choice what you do here in the play room. . . . I am here to help if you want . . . , however, there is something I want to say first. . . . I know you have had a very scary time in your family and you must be worried about what is happening to everyone.

(a glimmer of recognition from Shaun)

THERAPIST: . . . I know you are also living in a temporary place where you aren't very happy while various decisions are being made about the future . . . everything must feel very confusing . . . and nothing can be sorted out in a hurry . . . maybe we could concentrate on what feels the most important thing right now . . . such as the place where you are living now[3].

(Shaun looks directly at the therapist and then looks down, his eyes full with tears)

SHAUN: I hate it, I hate it (he mutters under his breath).

Teaching point

The naive therapist would perhaps want to find out what he hated – or might pre-suppose that it was only the incest he was talking about.

. . . there are four children in my room and one of them wets and it smells . . . and I sat on it once by mistake . . . and then I smelt.

Teaching point

Again, is this a metaphor? It may well be but also Shaun is describing something that has actually happened and that is causing him great distress.

THERAPIST: Could you draw a picture of where you live at the moment?

SHAUN: . . . No . . . I can't . . . if I draw it then it means it will be real and I don't want it to be real.

THERAPIST: We both know it will be real for a short time but not for a long time.

SHAUN: What is a short time? A few days?

THERAPIST: We can find out how long it is likely to be – but it will be several weeks not days.

SHAUN: Weeks not months? Not days but weeks? Lots of weeks? Can I just draw?

> **Teaching point**
>
> Notice how eloquent Shaun is when he says, 'Can I just draw?'. The home was something that he needed to talk about and the therapist was able to respond to him needing just to be in the now while these enormous changes were going on around him. The therapist and Shaun were able to negotiate a contract of four sessions where he could say and do whatever he felt like doing.

SHAUN (later):   when the big things happen . . . then we'll really need to talk . . . or play.

It is possible for some therapeutic work relating to abuse to become polarized: either the child feels, through therapy, that eventually it will be all right in this family, people can be forgiven and the family can come together again OR the child is encouraged to express all the outrage and anger without any recognition of other feelings that may exist towards the abuser and those who failed to protect the child.

> **Teaching point**
>
> There are some families that are too toxic for children to live in – and children should not have to feel permanently guilty about leaving such families. In other cases, there are other families where repair is possible both for the child and for the family as a whole. This may turn out to be a 'good enough' family rather than an 'ideal' family, but it will be one where there is enough basic protection for the child.

Statements such as the above are clear indications of why supervision is so important for the playtherapist's practice. When working with damaged children, it is all too easy to become involved in the child's experience and make judgements that are more to do with our own needs rather than the child's needs. As an example of this, in the wish for a family to change and accommodate a distressed child, are we perhaps talking about *our own family* and the distress that we experienced as a child?

If therapists feel outrage and indignation at the treatment of a child, is this anger on *behalf of the child* or is it our own anger? Murray Cox's reminder to therapists is very timely here – that we are *in* but not *of* the world of the patient (Cox, 1988). The needs of playtherapists themselves and the continuing importance of supervision are discussed in Chapter 9.

THE CHILD IN SHOCK

All children who come into therapy are, in their differing ways, in states of shock and trauma. However, the child who has experienced sudden and unexpected shock such as natural disasters, wars and serious crashes, has particular needs.

> 'It must be emphasised that stress is something determined subjectively by each individual according to assessment of the situation and past experiences. If the situation is translated as a threat to the individual, then stress will result. This threat need not necessarily be physical in nature, it could also be of three other basic types: a threat against one's family, friends or belongings; a threat against one's psychological integrity; and a threat against beliefs or values.'
>
> (Lahad, 1992)

We now understand more and more about post traumatic stress disorder (PTSD) in both children and adults. What is clear in the therapy offered in these situations is that explorations of the trauma are rarely the most effective way, certainly at the outset of therapy.

The threats or fear of threats against the individual as pointed out by Lahad, above, result in particular needs that have to be addressed. The following are usually the most immediate:

(1) The person needs to develop the capacity to self-soothe; to nurture themselves. They have lost this ability through guilt (I don't deserve to be cared for) or where there is actual loss of the carer (especially true for a child).

(2) The person needs to re-discover trusting relationship(s) which may begin in therapy and then generate out to other relationships. The therapist may well assist in that process through the symbolic play (see the case history of Penny below).

(3) The person needs to find support where they live through the

process of disillusionment and loss of belief that has been provoked by the trauma.

(4)   The person needs to externalize the trauma *in their own good time* – and not because the therapist thinks it may be a 'good thing'.

(5)   The person needs factual information – notice how important it was in the case of Penny below.

Case history

Penny, aged eight, was formally referred for playtherapy following crisis–fostering after the sudden death of her parents in a road accident. The foster parents reported that she was quiet, good, did not talk, did everything she was told and answered any questions in monosyllables. She did not respond to any physical contact. The school had reported similarly: that she was well behaved, carried out her work and did not join in playground games.

She came obediently into her playtherapy sessions, was shown all the materials, and responded 'yes, thank you' when asked if she understood what playtherapy was. Penny sat at the drawing table, took a pencil and paper, looked at the playtherapist and waited. The playtherapist suggested that she drew a garden and she produced the picture shown in Fig. 8.4. In response to being asked to describe her garden, she said 'There are the flowers, there is the grass, the sun is shining, there is a big tree – that's the gate to the garden.'

Teaching point

The inexperienced therapist might be tempted to weigh right in and ask 'Is the sun always shining?', thinking, quite rightly, that Penny has not been able to acknowledge when the sun set so tragically in her life. However, this would be premature – the key in this picture is the gate, as we shall see from the following intervention:

THERAPIST: 'Tell me about the gate.'

PENNY: 'The gate is locked – with a chain so that the garden stays safe – and then no-one will spoil the flowers'. She then looks at the therapist for the first time and says 'I want this garden to stay safe – and special.'

Fig. 8.4 Penny's garden.

Teaching point

What multiple metaphoric expression is in this brief description – and the therapist is being told quite explicitly how to
proceed. Don't open the gate – don't go into the garden –
keep it *safe and special*. The garden is herself and also her past
self when there were parents and life was secure – and maybe
it is also linked to their graves – the healing metaphor at this
point is the garden which is secure – not the garden to be
invaded, spoiled or destroyed.

With the acknowledgement of the safe garden, Penny was able to
express other things through different media. She constructed her foster

family with the dolls' house and told a story about the 'new family' – 'and the old girl was sad to be in a new family because the old family had gone – but they were kind.'

Penny had been to the funeral and knew about the car accident – so it seemed appropriate to say:

THERAPIST: 'and the old girl had had such a shock because the old family had gone so suddenly.'
PENNY (looking at the therapist with fear in her eyes): 'they were crushed, weren't they?'

Although her parents had died instantly in a collision, it turned out that Penny had overheard someone say, 'they must have been crushed to death – the fire engine had to cut them out.'

Teaching point

The therapist is now wondering whether to follow the child into the everyday reality that Penny is describing, or to guide her back into the metaphoric reality of the story that Penny has been telling about the old and the new family.
THERAPIST: 'The old girl is still shocked because no-one exactly explained how the old Mummy and Daddy died (Penny slowly shakes her head). The old Mummy and Daddy died immediately the two cars crashed – and the cars had to be separated by the firemen . . . and the old girl was sad for a long time.'
PENNY (with eyes full of tears):   'a long, long time.' (She put her head on her arms and started to cry.)

This example illustrates the many sub-texts that abound in such a situation and how the therapist *must* test the water with the child at each major step. In the situation above, the therapist chose to stay with the metaphor that the child had established in relation to 'the old family', 'the new family', and 'the old girl', and incorporated the fearful disclosure which, in turn, led into the first overt expression of grief.

Penny now began to ask questions about her parents' death from both her foster parents and her therapist; she gradually assimilated the real facts about their death. No-one can minimize the effects of sudden death – especially to a child (Papadatou & Papadatos, 1991). The next step for Penny was to be able to slowly work with her body and to allow physical touch; she was able to get into this through simple games in the soft area and by choosing one special soft toy to play with as her 'new friend'. There were also stories about the old girl and the new friend. The foster parents got in touch to say that Penny would now allow herself to be tucked up in bed – to actually have the bedclothes tucked in round her – and had asked if she could have a duvet like the other children. This links with her earlier expression about being crushed and the fact that her avoidance of physicality seemed to have its dominant roots in physical fear.

Teaching point

In such cases, it is crucial that the child receives clear communication and explanations about what is happening which take into account the following:

- Has too much information been given too soon – especially if the child is in shock?
- How much information can the child retain at one go?
- What language is being used to explain things to the child? (Avoid adult logic or 'mimsy' language that dresses up the situation or avoids the real issues.)
- Who else has communicated to the child – have things been overheard and misunderstood?
- Has anyone tried to say to the child to 'forget all about it' when the child has not had time to mourn or grieve?

CHILDREN WHO CANNOT PLAY

Children who have never been allowed or encouraged to play are quite overwhelmed when they come into a playtherapy situation (an example of this is the case history of Bobby given in Chapter 2). Most playtherapy rooms have so much choice and such a range of materials that a child can 'freeze' and be unable to begin.

It is important to first ascertain whether the child is unable to play because of developmental difficulties: due to early hospitalization, for example, family trauma, or belief system, or whether there is organic damage which has impeded the usual learning stages. In cases where there is brain damage as well as prolonged hospitalization, the play processes are likely to take that much longer.

Case history

I was called into a Special Education Unit in Eastern Europe to advise on play activities for children with brain damage; the existing equipment consisted of classical educational toys – wooden peg-boards; stacking shapes and rings; 'posting' shapes. Three girls sat at a table sorting glass beads into triangular sections in a round box. A younger boy, hyperactive, scampered around the room touching and dropping different equipment; he came to the table, grabbed a handful of beads – paused a moment – and flung them across the room, to the amusement of the three girls and the despair of the teacher. One bead had dropped on the table so I knelt down and blew it across to the other side of the table: the boy stopped in his tracks and watched: he then promptly moved opposite me and tried to blow the bead back. After several attempts he succeeded and we developed a simple game of blowing the bead and then flicking the bead to each other; we then found it impossible to blow two beads at once, so we started lining the beads up according to their colour. The head teacher said that the boy had never been still since he had arrived at the school.

Many children are able to start at the beginning of their EPR stages and to work through them with the therapist taking care that the activities are age-appropriate in terms of preventing the children from feeling stupid. It is worth repeating that it is important not to bombard a child with stimulus. The situation can be contained within one small space – the table or the sandbox; or one medium – sand or Plasticine; or one physical activity – rolling in different ways.

A child who is prevented from playing by the family who sees such activity as 'silly' or 'a waste of time', again needs a careful approach. The playtherapist is in effect giving permission for something that is not allowed at home and the child's value system will be in conflict. Peter Slade's guidelines (1954) for balancing the proportions of 'personal play and projective play' are important ones. Personal play involves the whole person – the child as actor is important for developing confidence and sociability; projective play, as well as being a medium for therapeutic expression, also enables the shy or withdrawn child to work safely within the technique and not take risks either physically or in role. The 'pocket therapist' described earlier, where the playtherapist works in miniature, can also be a way to engage with the reluctant child.

The child who has not been allowed to play can be in a situation similar to that of the child who won't allow him or herself to play. With the former, the parents are exercising external control and in the latter the child is imposing internal control.

Yet another challenging situation arise with the very controlled child who is absolutely terrified of play and the seeming chaos that can result. It is important for the playtherapist not to impose a norm of playful behaviour but to allow for the individuality of the child within the range of diverse playing.

For the playtherapist, it is important to check out both the class and cultural norms regarding child development and play activity. Too often, for example, racial variation can be interpreted as pathology.

Learning not to make assumptions

A nursery nurse student on placement chose to work with traveller children in a school near a traveller site. The student thought that playtherapy could be used to make the bridge between home and the school and to express possible conflicts non-verbally. She arranged to work both with a small group of four children and with one child individually. In her supervision she was very distressed that all the children simply refused to play as she had expected and sat at the table wanting to do lessons. I suggested that she did some background work on traveller families before making any assumptions about the failure of the playtherapy. She discovered that traveller children who may well play freely out of doors, and be very inventive and creative with a whole range of media, are very different indoors. To them, the idea of taking off shoes and socks and sitting on the floor inside is anathema. This finding triggered a more detailed investigation into the complex set of rules and taboos surrounding the traveller belief system – one that is as complex as any other cultural or racial group.

Much of the Temiar data that I gathered in Malaysia made a lot more sense once I realized that the Temiar's spatial system is divided up into those activities that can take place on the ground and those that must take place off the ground (Jennings, 1992). Children are not allowed on the ground until they can walk independently. This is usually the time they are given their proper name – before they can walk they will have been known simply as 'boy' or 'girl'. From about the age of seven or eight, children no longer sleep with no near their parents but with their own peer group. Groups of seven- and eight-year-olds decide whose house they will sleep in on any particular evening. It was very difficult for me as a Western mother to allow my own eight-year-old to sleep with his peer group in different houses and I always remember my own initial discomfort on these occasions as a guideline for not making assumptions about other cultures and belief systems. Equally, the playtherapist should always check what may be a perfectly ordinary explanation before assuming there is abnormality or disturbance: in other words, *ask the child*.

Teaching point

The playtherapist always has to balance the various factors before making assumptions about pathology and remember the story of the child sent for assessment who raced and jumped down stairs after going to the lavatory. When asked why he did it, he replied that he wanted to reach the bottom of the stairs before the water filled up again – in other words, this was a piece of playacting, a child's game.

THE OCCURRENCE OF NIGHTMARES

The playtherapist should make sure that he or she is clear about the development of anxiety (free floating) and fear (located). Parents should understand the various routines that can contain and change nightmare patterns. Children depend on the care of parents to survive so it is important that where possible the parents themselves can intervene to transform the fearful dream.

If a child comes to playtherapy because of nightmares it is important to start with an open contract, that is the parents, therapist and child know why the child has come. The nightmare can be drawn and painted, modelled in Plasticine or clay, or built in the sandtray with sand and water. It can be played out through the toys, through puppets and through dramatic play, and through story telling. The child may need to move from one medium to another and to work the nightmare through in several ways. The child needs to find power to deal with the nightmare – to disempower the monster; the child may play the role of the monster, for example, in dramatic play. If the child draws a frightening monster together with a little child, progress to telling the story through the pictures. The child can play the role of the monster; the therapist can then play the child and ask questions in order to bring about change. A nightmare may need to be worked at several times at intervals in order to bring about a decrease in its power. *If a nightmare persists after working through in therapy or if a new nightmare appears, check for other possibilities such as abuse.*

Among the range of playtherapy equipment, make sure you have plenty of monster toys – space monsters, prehistoric monsters, monster slime. Have very small versions of them too as a way for the child to take control and reduce their power. There are many stories about overcoming monsters, both old and new, that can be read, dramatized or modelled.

Case history

Susan had a waking nightmare having read in an old book of her uncle's the story of Richard III murdering the little princes in the tower. She woke at night crying, and remembered much of the story verbatim, 'and the little princes looked like two pale flowers on the pillow.' She wanted her parents to destroy the book and when they demurred, made them lock it away in a cupboard. The book itself needed to be contained. The therapy consisted of a very brief intervention as she talked about how the story had frightened her, and how sorry she felt for the princes to be murdered by their uncle. I asked her directly if she was frightened of the uncle who had given her the book and she said that she wasn't but that she had never met him and didn't know who he was because the family did not approve of him.

Susan needed to talk through the story and her fear in daylight and to be able to understand her genuine feelings of grief at the death of these children through their very graphic story together with the book's pictures. She was learning about the reality of death. She then asked for her book back because it represented an important link with this uncle she did not and would not know.

CHILDREN WHO CANNOT ALLOW TOUCH

I would like to end this chapter with suggestions for dealing with the child who avoids any touch at all costs in the playtherapy. Some therapists believe that touch should not be a part of the therapy, that the therapist should be outside the physical orbit of the child, and that the media and toys are the means of contact taking place. The Playtherapy Method includes a range of physical techniques, many of which involve touch. Most children's play and games involve varying degrees of touch and I regard it as artificial not to allow this as part of the therapeutic value of the play. Obviously the therapist both exercises care in the choice of methods and is scrupulously honest about his or her personal motives. Many playtherapists now videotape their sessions in order to protect themselves should there at any stage be misunderstanding of their intervention.

However much we may feel that appropriate touching is healthful and therapeutic, there are some children who totally refuse to touch or to allow touch and who will always set up physical distance between themselves and the therapist. It is as if the child has drawn a large circle of personal space around his or her body and does not want this to be violated.

In these cases the playtherapist needs to experiment. It may mean in the early days that the child plays at a distance so long as the therapist does not get 'too close'. The therapist can bridge the space by continuing to talk to the child while at the same time respecting the space. Walkie-talkies and telephones are useful ways of bridging the distance vocally. Container play – as described in earlier chapters – allows symbolic safety and both child and therapist can play in containers. String, streamers and 'falls' (beautiful long strips of chiffon available from sari shops) can all serve to make contact. This is like establishing an intermediary between adult and child (I do not think that this necessarily establishes a symbolic umbilical cord!).

The child who does not want to touch will sometimes show violence towards toys in the playtherapy environment. It is important to be clear with the child about ground rules here – and whether some things can be knocked about or not. It may be that a child is so terrified of his or her own potential violence that he or she will not allow the touch of other people. One little girl, for example, had been told repeatedly, 'You'll be the death of me' by her mother.

SUMMARY

This chapter has dealt with some of the more difficult situations playtherapists may have to face in their work. It has also addressed some of the realities of playtherapy in practice, starting with the clear contract and expectations that are set up with the child and the family. Attention has been drawn to how children are assessed and referred and the importance of role clarity. Cross cultural beliefs and racial variation have been commented upon. Suggestions have been made for working with more difficult problems, such as child abuse, the child who cannot or will not play, and the child who has nightmares.

The importance of hearing the child and not making assumptions about interpretations or pathology is emphasized.

NOTES

[1]   The play and the characters in 'Hamlet' are a useful family study for anyone working as a therapist: the ambivalence about the ghost, for example, whether it is from heaven or hell; and Hamlet's feelings about what he sees as the incest of his mother. My own thinking is that Ophelia was probably anorectic and committed suicide as the only way of having a voice, having struggled so much with the control of both her father and her brother (Jennings, in preparation).

[2]   The question here is: is the playtherapist doing disclosure work or therapeutic work? These roles have to be kept differentiated and separate. If disclosure happens in the course of therapy then the supervisor will be able to guide the playtherapist on the best course of action (usually, the fact that confidentiality can be broken if there is a danger to client or other covers most contingencies).

[3]   Notice how the therapist does not call the new place 'home' and acknowledges the distress of the child without going into any detail. Children have very strong feelings about places they do not feel to be 'home' and people who they do not want to call 'parent'.

REFERENCES

Cattanach, A. (1992) *Play Therapy with Abused Children*. London: Jessica Kingsley.

Cox, M. (1989) *Structuring the Therapeutic Process: Compromise with Chaos*. London: Jessica Kingsley.

Jennings, S. (Ed) (1992) *Dramatherapy, Theory and Practice 2*. London: Routledge.

Lahad, M. (1992) 'Story Making in Assessment Methods for Coping with Stress: six-piece story-making and BASIC Ph'. In *Dramatherapy Theory and Practice 2* (Ed. S. Jennings). London: Routledge.

Slade, P. (1954) *Child Drama*. London: University of London Press.

Chapter 9

Playtherapy Resources

'She can't get angry', little My said. 'That's
what's wrong with her.' 'Listen, you,' My
continued and went close to Ninny with a
menacing look. 'You'll never have a face
of your own until you've learned to fight.
Believe me.'

The story of 'The Invisible Child' from
Tales from Moominvalley, T. Janssen.

I have deliberately chosen to devote a chapter to resources and the
playtherapy milieu rather than put the material and information
into an appendix. I hope that this will underline the necessity of
appropriate resources and the central importance of an adequate
environment and media for professional playtherapy practice. Too
often staff are asked to undertake playtherapy without consideration of such things as:

- Environment: i.e. the shape and size of room; floor covering;
  privacy
- Time: both for assessment and practice, as well as planning and
  recording
- Media and materials, including range and choice
- Supervision, consultation, support and training

What can be considered the ideal requirements form the substance
of this chapter, but consideration will also be given to working
with a modest budget and the provision of basic essentials which
should not have to be compromised.

THE PLAYTHERAPY ENVIRONMENT

A playtherapy space should be single purpose: warm, light and airy, with a view of the world beyond. Carpets are not advisable since they cause carpet-burns during movement and do not give a child a feeling of immediate support. Woodblock or cork tiles are preferable, with non-slip mats in some areas. The room should be divided into several areas for different forms of play and have some larger equipment that is replaced as appropriate. The following are some examples:

- A soft area with a play mattress, cushions, pillows and blankets
- A wet area for sand and water play, with water, clay and mess
- A toy area for playing with different sorts of toys;
- A drama area for games and drama
- A drawing and painting area with tables
- A quiet area for storytelling and reflection

The soft area: a safe place for energetic physical games; jumping and rolling; hiding and sleeping. It can also be combined with the drama area (below) to create scenarios for enactment and dramatic play. It needs a number of soft toys and cushions of different shapes, sizes and colours that can be sat upon, built with, and used in a variety of ways during physical activities.

The wet area: needs a basin with hot and cold water, water and sand containers, a clay table and chairs.

The toy area: should have sturdy containers for different sets and groupings of toys; building materials and a dolls' house. Shelves may contain wooden boxes and plastic stacking bowls.

The drama area: this can be combined with the soft area and should have a simple climbing frame for creating houses or towers and a barrel to crawl into.

The drawing and painting area: should be near the wet area, with tables to sit or stand at for painting work.

The quiet area: this should be a calm and still area where a child can listen to a story; wind down from a session and reflect; or 'de-role' from the dramatic engagement before a session finishes. It needs a mat and cushions or chairs.

Interior decoration

The walls of the playtherapy room should be painted in light rather than bright colours, with a selection of posters and pictures that are not stereotypical or prejudicial in relation to gender, race or class. If the ceiling is high, an inexpensive false ceiling can be created with cross slats. Strip lighting should not be used. Concealed spotlights, which illuminate different areas in different ways, are the most appropriate. The room should also have sturdy, lockable cupboards for a child's own materials to be kept in. The main door should lock, but be able to be entered from the outside in emergencies; there should be an alarm system. The floor should be sealed to enable easy wiping and cleaning and to avoid the use of plastic covering.

When such a space is not available – as, for example, when a room is multi-purpose – then certain issues must be addressed. The room must then be available on a regular basis for therapy sessions, with sufficient time for preparation and clearing up. It must be private and not be part of a thoroughfare or have people knocking on the door or any other sort of interruption. However small the space it should have contrasting areas even if this is simply a quiet area with an action area with water play in a washing up bowl in one corner. Children's play-work which they wish to keep must have storage space that is locked and safe.

Ann Cattanach, one of my colleagues, spends some of her time working as a playtherapist in situ. She creates the space by taking with her a blue carpet (Cattanach, 1992) and equipment in different sorts of bags. Whether the space is permanent or mobile, it must have the potential for creating a space that is different – a magical and symbolic space where things can be *allowed*. There are many feelings and thoughts that a child needs to feel safe to express and that cannot be expressed in any other space.

MEDIA AND MATERIALS

With the plethora of play equipment available it is very difficult for playtherapists to be able to have a balanced range of equipment within their budget. It is important to check the following:

- Is the budget 'start-up' money (and therefore not to be repeated)?
- What about funding for consumables?
- Do other people have use of the equipment?
- Who is responsible for cleaning, tidying, mending and generally overseeing the equipment?
- Is there any variation in standards of maintenance? You may find that the way you maintain the equipment is different from other staff (rather as in families!) and this can cause friction and resentment
- See if you can find a friendly printer who will allow you regular supplies of ends of rolls
- Try not to confuse 'junk materials' for creating and exploring, with 'rubbish equipment' where everything is cracked, broken, or has pieces missing
- Be sure to check the safety standard, i.e. toxicity of paint; eyes of soft toys; badly made toys; splinters, and so on
- Make sure that there are aprons, old shirts and smocks in order to protect the child's personal clothing

Soft toys (Fig. 9.1)

Large, small, and very small soft, furry, cuddly toys (even teddy bears as big as a child) can be bought for under £20. However, beware of fire hazards and cheap fur that can stick up noses and down throats and irritate eyes. Good fabric departments stock a large choice of fur fabrics from which many different toys can be made.

Dolls' house

This should be an open fronted dolls' house with a range of furniture that is as flexible as possible. There are wooden building sets that can be made into a dolls' house, as well as be turned into other buildings. You may want to have a second dolls' house which can be used for destructive/aggressive play. Beware of using stereotyped dolls.

Small animals (Fig. 9.2)

You can make a large collection of animals which include those on farms, zoos and those found in the wild. Include baby animals as

Fig. 9.1 A collection of soft toys.

well as the adults, and make sure there are land, water and air creatures. Include trees, gates, fences and cages as part of the collection.

Tiny toys

The very small toys described in Chapter 5 come into this category, i.e. a miniature Punch and Judy, nursery rhyme and fairytale figures, etc. Tiny families (sleep dolls) can be found in charity

Fig. 9.2 A family of small elephants.

shops or made from pipe cleaners. Baby animals can also be used here as well as magic 'jewels'.

Educational toys

A large range of wooden and plastic construction toys can be useful in the playtherapy room, especially to encourage mastery skills and improve confidence. There is also a point where educational play coincides with therapeutic play and one experience feeds into the other.

Water play

A collection of useful objects includes a large water container with cups and saucers, funnels, sprays, feeding bottles and a water pistol.

Sandplay

Install a large container of sand (or use a tray or bowl), and use sand specifically refined for play. Sand may be mixed with water and used for building, tunnelling and decorating. Chapter 1 includes a description of the particular forms of sand play used by Jungian child therapists, and particular use of sandplay and toys can also be found in the 'World Technique' section of that chapter.

Drawing and painting

Acquire a range of large 'jumbo' crayons, charcoal and oil-based crayons, finger paint in primary colours, paints and large brushes and ample supplies of different sorts of paper.

Junk play

Collect cardboard boxes of all sizes (from fridge packaging to shoebox) for drama work and for creating 'journey boxes' or 'sense boxes' (see Chapter 5). Large boxes can become houses, castles and tunnels. They can also be built into totem poles, trees and bridges. Whole environments can be created from waste materials: shredded computer paper, newspaper, container rolls (although to use toilet roll middles is perhaps taking the notion of junk too far).

Fabric scraps of different textures and shapes are also useful: small pieces can be used for artwork/sculpting; larger pieces for dressing-up self and toys. Good quality material can be obtained from manufacturers and from the wardrobe departments of large theatres.

Leaves, twigs, grasses, straw and flowers can also be combined with sandplay or used with other types of play materials.

Nesting dolls

Russian dolls (Babushkas) come in several shapes and sizes. Traditional-style peasant women with red head-scarves are available and it is now possible to buy variations on this theme – ethnic dolls in saris and male as well as female doll sets.

Puppets

Glove and finger puppets are probably the most frequently used puppets in playtherapy. It is possible to obtain three-generational families of finger puppets and a variety of animals that are easy for small fingers to handle. Glove puppets can be made from gloves or socks, or from papier mâché or fur fabric. Some puppets are too clumsy or heavy for small hands to manage.

Very small finger puppets can be used for 'tiny play' like other very small toys. A child can thus contain a whole family on the fingers of one hand.

Dolls

Baby dolls can be used for bathing, dressing and undressing, and putting to bed. Other dolls can be used for family play. Some children prefer to work with dolls'-house-size dolls; others find that these are too tiny for easy use and choose to work in a larger dimension. The dolls can be combined with the soft toys for family and situation-play and storytelling.

Books

A range of suitable books should cover stories that can be used therapeutically as well as stories for health that can be read to children as part of the therapy. There are stories that can be painted, dramatized and improvised, and stories that can have new endings created for them. The playtherapist needs a rich fund of stories from their own experience to draw on and these should include stories from many different cultures.

Music

Musical instruments are an important part of the playroom – bongo drums, cymbals, penny whistles and chime bars are essential basics and can be easily developed. Some playtherapists use taped music (and sound effects), but generally live music is preferable, particularly since many children are de-sensitized to music through experience of loud non-stop, undifferentiated sound.

PROFESSIONAL PRACTICE

Time management

With the pressure of modern living and the demands on play-therapists' time, it is often difficult to allow enough time for clients and therapists to maximize opportunities within the therapeutic setting. Playtherapists also often fall into the trap (often set by senior colleagues) of 'would you just . . .':

* Write this report
* Complete this assessment
* Take on this emergency client
* Attend this review

Most playtherapists also have difficulty saying 'no'! The personality and attitudes of playtherapists is more fully discussed in Chapter 10 but it is pertinent to mention them here in order to underline the realities of structuring time.

A good guide to follow is to remember that however long a session may last (for example, thirty-five minutes for infants, up to fifty minutes for older children), at least that amount of time again is needed for planning and recording the session. Furthermore, there should be gaps between sessions to allow the therapist to de-role and distance from current therapeutic materials, so that he or she may freshly engage with the next client.

One complete session should allow time for engaging with the client and developing the work and at least a third of the time for reflection, de-roling, distancing and disengagement. The closure of a session is as important as the opening: it is through the closure that a child will experience safety and containment, and so sufficient time should always be allowed.

Supervision

It is more important for a playtherapist to have regular supervision than to have a large equipment budget. Supervision requires a clearly defined relationship between supervisor and supervisee where the supervised therapist is able to reflect on his or her interventions with clients. The situation often mirrors the client/therapist situation and the supervisee is able to gain insight into his or her feelings, choices and ways of working through exploring this relationship. Supervisors need to have extensive experience of working with children and to be sympathetic to playtherapy practice. The supervisor should have no other roles in relation to the supervisee (such as line management, personal therapist, and so on), since this would bring about role confusion and in turn affect the work with the child. There must be mutual respect between supervisee and supervisor and uninterrupted time for regular meetings. Supervision time as well as finance should be the responsibility of the employer; in other words the playtherapist's job description should include sufficient resources to allow for supervision.

Consultation

Playtherapists should have recourse to adequate consultation with appropriate practitioners concerning their practice. However experienced a supervisor, for example, consultation may be necessary in relation to child abuse. Finally, all playtherapy practice should have adequate clinical monitoring on a regular basis.

Support

The first line of support for the playtherapist must come from the agency itself. There can be some envy and jealousy from colleagues who may denigrate playtherapy and who may not fully understand it. One colleague, for example, was made to feel very de-skilled when greeted by a colleague in front of other staff with, 'It's your tambourine session, is it?'

Support, therefore, must come from the agency itself. It must be stated in policy and practice that playtherapy is a recognized and important form of intervention. It should be supported by adequate resources and also by other colleagues. A regular staff support group can give mutual support for the team; however, a support group should not be confused with a supervision group.

Training

It is important to realize that playtherapists will always have training needs. They need to be able to replenish their skills; they also need to be able to gain experience and work with other practitioners and have opportunities for skill sharing and development.

Although playtherapists will have had extended personal therapy in their training, it is also the case that many will choose to go back into personal therapy, especially when painful client materials have touched areas in their own lives.

Research and publishing

Much research still needs to be undertaken in playtherapy theory and method and playtherapists should be encouraged to undertake this and to publish their findings. There is now a professional association which supports and represents the interests of playtherapists, and it is hoped that in time it will expand nationwide. There is a wealth of different areas of expertise that could contribute to such a body and help refine and develop the field for the future.

REFERENCES

Cattanach, A. (1992) 'Playtherapy and dramatic play with young children who have been abused'. In *Dramatherapy Theory and Practice 2* (Ed. S. Jennings). London: Routledge.

Jennings, S. (1990) *Dramatherapy with Families, Groups and Individuals.* London: Jessica Kingsley.

Janssen, T. (1973) *Tales from Moominvalley.* London: Puffin.

Chapter 10

The Playtherapist – Current Expectations

Our view of the role and expectations of the person expected to play therapeutically with children is often ambivalent and confused. First, society has conflicting views on the value of play in human development (despite the wealth of writing and research) and secondly it is often seen as something we 'grow out of'. In addition, the education system progressively reduces the amount of playful possibilities as children grow older. By secondary education, virtually all play is limited to organized sports and games: sports and games, however, are just one dimension of play activity. The arts offer a whole area of necessary play activity for human beings. Nevertheless this aspect of the arts is underdeveloped and they are not given fundamental priority either in education or in society at large.

There tends to be a gulf between the role of the person who is trained to play with children and that of the person who is trained to 'do therapy' with children. People who engage in play, such as nursery school teachers and nursery nurses, also undergo a shorter training period than other children's professionals. On the other hand, playgroup leaders, activity organizers, holiday project managers and so on, need no qualification at all. By contrast with these two groups, child psychotherapists who incorporate play into psychotherapy, are required to have an extensive training over a period of four or more years. Between these various polarities, come social workers, teachers, paediatric occupational therapists, and nurses: all have some experience of and brief training in play and its use in assessment, diagnosis and therapeutic practice, but here the skill is one among many.

In order to properly appraise the situation, there needs to be a fundamental change in thinking in relation to play. Play is not merely an activity for which the most important requirement is to supervise children while they play with the right equipment. If the ability to play is necessary for human survival and adult living, as we discussed in the earlier chapters of this book, then re-education needs to take place at all levels of our society, not only with professionals, but also with parents and families. What we see, however, is a decrease of resources for pre-school playgroups and social service provision at a time when the plight of more and more damaged children is being highlighted. Waiting lists for child psychotherapy lengthen; most psychotherapy for children is long-term treatment.

BRINGING PLAY AND THERAPY TOGETHER

One step that can be made in our thinking is to bring together the words play and therapy – as this book has done. We can observe the play of all children, including if we have them our own, and see that in itself it is therapeutic. Situations can be tested, fears played out, skills practised, fantasy developed, spontaneity and imagination stimulated, and rules and outcome experienced and learned. Those activities are all healthy, educational and therapeutic, and part of all normal development. Within areas that are defined as 'at risk' for various reasons – whether in families, situations (such as hospital) or geographical areas – there should be increased play provision. Such 'preventative play' could enable individuals to build up additional resources to deal with difficult situations.

If as a society we can see that all play is therapeutic *as well as* educational, it becomes easier to understand its importance as a *therapy* for those children (and adults too) who are deprived, damaged or otherwise cut off from normal play experience. *All play, though playful, is also a very serious activity and needs to be taken seriously.*

In addition, if we can bring together these two concepts of therapy and education and see them as directly relating to each other, it becomes easier to formulate an understanding of who should be practising playtherapy.

SOME TRAINING AND EXPERIENTIAL GUIDELINES

It is obvious that those professionals who are going to enter the playtherapy field need additional training and experience. It is not enough to understand theories of play; it is also essential to be able to engage in play. The guidelines given below have evolved over many years of developing training for playtherapists (see also Appendix 3).

The first important guideline to remember is that if we are going to be able to play with children, we must also be able to play ourselves as adults. We need to enjoy playing in all its dimensions and to value it in our own lives. *A person cannot be an effective playtherapist if he or she is unable to play freely as an adult.*

All of us have areas in our own childhood that were difficult, painful, fearful or stressed, as I illustrated in the introduction. Who we are as an adult is influenced by our own internal child. This inner child forms part of our adult identity and forms a large part of the way in which we relate to other children. A playtherapist needs, therefore, to have explored in therapy their own lives, with a particular focus on their own childhood experience. *In order to maximize our capacity to work as a playtherapist, it is necessary to have an extended time in personal playtherapy ourselves.*

If this preparation does not take place then we are in danger of making use of playtherapy practice as a way of resolving our own difficulties.

The practice of playtherapy can make enormous demands on the playtherapist. People's attitudes towards those who work in play can be, 'aren't you lucky to be paid for playing?', or, 'Is playing with children really a job . . . a proper job?', or, 'Mary isn't too bright so she is going to work with children'; the reality is that playtherapy taxes a person at every level – physically, mentally, emotionally and spiritually. How does a playtherapist deal with their own feelings when they witness the story of an infant that has been repeatedly sexually abused or physically assaulted almost to the point of death? *A playtherapist needs enormous stamina and resilience at all levels of experience.*

Some people who work in playtherapy do so out of a sense of mission; of a need to help the victim. They see themselves as championing the right of the child, often *against* the adult. *The playtherapist is not substituting for damaged parenting, but rather is an intermediary or agency through whom the child can resolve difficulties.*

In order to understand children within a social and family context, it is important for playtherapists to have experience of different family cultures within society and to have insight into the role of the perpetrator of child violence and abuse. However, when I have suggested that all people working with victims of child physical and sexual abuse should have experience of working with the perpetrators, I have been greeted with some horrified reactions. *Playtherapists need to have experience of families where damage has occurred, particularly with perpetrators of abuse in order to understand the issues in a context, however 'bad' or 'evil' we may feel the deeds have been.*

Perhaps I could ask the reader to consider the following speech from Shakespeare's *Macbeth* (Act I scene 7, lines 31–77), particularly the words spoken by Lady Macbeth, as an introduction to understanding the perpetrator, who it turns out, is also a victim:

MACBETH
>   We will proceed no further in this business.
>   He hath honoured me of late, and I have bought
>   Golden opinions from all sorts of people
>   Which would be worn now in their newest gloss,
>   Not cast aside so soon.

LADY MACBETH
>   Was the hope drunk
>   Wherein you dressed yourself? Hath it slept since?
>   And wakes it now to look so green and pale
>   At what it did so freely? From this time
>   Such I account thy love. Art thou afeard
>   To be the same in thine own act and valour
>   As thou art in desire? Wouldst thou have that
>   Which thou esteem'st the ornament of life,
>   And live a coward in thine own esteem,
>   Letting 'I dare not' wait upon 'I would',
>   Like the poor cat i' the adage?

MACBETH
>   Prithee peace.
>   I dare do all that may become a man;
>   Who dares do more is none.

LADY MACBETH
>   What beast was't then
>   That made you break this enterprise to me?
>   When you durst do it, then you were a man;
>   And to be more than what you were, you would
>   Be so much more the man. Nor time nor place
>   Did then adhere, and yet you would make both.
>   They have made themselves, and that their fitness now

Does unmake you. I have given suck, and know
How tender 'tis to love the babe that milks me;
I would while it was smiling in my face
Have plucked my nipple from his boneless gums
And dashed the brains out, had I so sworn as you
Have done to this.

MACBETH

If we should fail?

LADY MACBETH

We fail!

But screw your courage to the sticking place,
And we'll not fail. When Duncan is asleep –
Whereto the rather shall his day's hard journey
Soundly invite him – his two chamberlains
Will I with wine and wassail so convince
That memory, the warder of the brain,
Shall be a-fume, and the receipt of reason
A limbeck only. When in swinish sleep
Their drenched natures lies as in a death,
What cannot you and I perform upon
The unguarded Duncan? What not put upon
His spongy officers, who shall bear the guilt
Of our great quell?

MACBETH

Bring forth men-children only!
For thy undaunted mettle should compose
Nothing but males. Will it not be received,
When we have marked with blood those sleepy two
Of his own chamber, and used their very daggers,
That they have done't?

As discussed in Chapter 9 *resources should be made available so that
all playtherapists can have appropriate supervision either individually or in
small groups with a trained supervisor.*

Much of the therapeutic work that is available for children is
short- to medium-term intervention. Resources are either not available for long-term therapy, or it is not seen as necessarily the
most appropriate intervention. However, short-term work, in itself, places particular demands on therapists who often feel their
endeavours thwarted or work unfulfilled: 'If only I could have seen
the child for longer' is a common cry. I do not disagree that many
children do need longer term help, but there is also a kind of
privileged 'hierarchy' that has built up around all long-term therapy
(whether psychoanalysis with adults or children, or long-term psy-

chotherapy). There is often an implicit assumption that short-term therapy is somehow less worthy – not really 'true' therapy. The result of this is that those people who undertake short-term intervention often feel they are not 'real therapists', or that they do not have a voice in the case conference regarding a child's future.

As an example of this, at one such meeting, a playtherapist colleague of mine who had undertaken some extremely delicate work with a boy of nine who was already sexually abusing (not just indulging in sexual play) children younger than himself, was asked (by a child psychoanalyst): 'How about if you continue for a little while longer and then we can think about starting some real therapy?'

Whether playtherapy is undertaken for two sessions or twenty, the playtherapist needs to be valued for the serious work that is being undertaken and to be able to give serious input into the considerations of the welfare and future of the child.

KEEPING ALIVE OUR ABILITY TO PLAY

One of the problems of working in the caring or helping professions is that it not only becomes the central focus of our working lives but also very often our private lives as well. Time is taken outside work to attend extra courses, conferences, evening classes and supervision, and many work settings are unhelpful in understanding the necessary time needed *within the work time* for additional training and enhancement of skills.

Employers of playtherapists need an understanding of the resources of time and funding for additional training and continuing supervision of playtherapists once they are trained and in post.

Playtherapists in particular need to have the time and opportunity to play freely for themselves and not just because it is a part of their work. We need to continually discover the delights and frustrations of our own creative playing, in whatever form we choose to do this. It may be through sports and games, for example, or attendance at evening classes in craft, art, poetry or drama. Do we regard our cooking and gardening as creative playful activities or are they 'obligations'? If we do not find them creative then we need to have other media and means through which we can continue to explore this part of ourselves. Do we always bath in a hurry? Perhaps we could remember to take extra time to enjoy the water and bubbles, to use bath-toys or massage cream. I have taken a personal delight in the fact that for three successive Christmas presents, one of my adult sons has given me soap shaped like peas in a pod, monster 'slime' bubble bath and Ninja Turtle bubble bath.

Every adult needs to find their own source of play individually and in groups, and to feel able to put aside time for these activities without feelings of guilt. It is an age-old joke that parents give their children toys they would like to play with themselves. Perhaps all parents should give themselves these toys and not purloin those of their children. *All playtherapists need to have regular play and creative time that is not undertaken on behalf of their work.*

Many of the activities suggested here include what we refer to as 'the arts': music, dance, drama and visual arts; I refer to the *art and craft* of play. *Artistic activity for the playtherapist is an important development in their creative process which is inherent in all playful activity.*

We can now summarize the areas of training and experience that are important for playtherapists:

- Extended practise at different forms of play
- Theoretical understanding of developmental psychology and theories of play and child therapy
- An understanding of the relationship between play and the arts, especially in relation to dramatic play and drama
- Personal experience in therapy as a client – this pays attention to the person's 'inner child' and childhood experience
- Understanding and experience of family and cultural contexts
- Access to regular supervision of practice
- Opportunities for personal play within own life-style

ROLE CONFLICT FOR THE PLAYTHERAPIST

Many people who undertake playtherapy find that they adopt several roles in relation to the children with whom they work and that this can often get in the way of therapeutic intervention. Residential social work settings and children's homes, for example, often use a system of each child having a 'key worker' who is also expected to undertake playtherapy.

The first step here is to be aware of potential role conflict; where multiple roles are unavoidable, the role-relationships should be structured in such a way that child and therapist are both clear what is going on. For example, the playtherapy space needs to be a place set apart, as described in Chapter 9, so that the child knows that the therapeutic intervention and any discussions are contained in that space and will not overspill into day-to-day situations. Key workers often feel themselves to be in the role of temporary foster-parents, and have difficulties in dealing with issues of attachment and dependency. These issues can also enter the playtherapy setting and get in the way of therapeutic intervention. Skilled supervision is the only way for these difficulties to be addressed.

Playtherapists are often asked to undertake 'disclosure work' to be used in assessment and potential legal proceedings. It is of paramount importance that the same person whose brief it is to do disclosure work is not also working as the child's playtherapist in treatment. Major confusions of confidentiality arise and the therapist working in treatment is put under pressure to get information disclosed that can be used in evidence.

Teams who work with children need not only supervision for playtherapy practice but also group supervision and clinical monitoring to enhance effective communication and improve the total care and provision for the child. This leads onto the question of the multi-professional team and its scope for addressing the needs of children with problems.

THE MULTI-PROFESSIONAL TEAM

It is difficult to get a sense of unity in relation to children when there can be so many agencies involved. For example, social services, education, the police, the foster-parents, the child and family centre, can all be involved at any one time and many at one-and-the-same time. An adequate working structure needs to be formulated in order for conflict of interest and practice to be avoided.

It is useful to ask the following:

- Who is responsible for the child's primary care?
- If this is not the family of origin, how are links and contact maintained and through whom?
- Who is responsible for therapeutic assessment?
- Who is responsible for the child's therapy?
- Who takes responsibility for possible ensuing court procedures?
- How does this relate to the child's school and educational needs?
- How does this relate to any medical treatment that is necessary?

- Who checks out that the child is still developing a peer and social life as far as possible?

With the extreme pressures that exist on local authorities and various agencies, it is often the case that various groups are all taking action that this is not necessarily compatible. *All of this practice should be available for external consultation and supervision where necessary, without staff feeling vulnerable or de-skilled.*

CLOSING THOUGHTS

In the light of the implementation of the Children Act 1989 there is much polemic and debate as to the nature of children's wishes. The media offer a platform to discussion groups, often in heated opposition to each other, as to the needs of children and where the decision-making does or should take place. Parents and other agencies must make certain decisions regarding the care and welfare of the child – that goes without saying. However, these decisions need to take into account how a child is feeling, perceiving and experiencing the world. Sometimes we can only find that information through a medium such as playtherapy. Children do not necessarily have ready answers in response to questions from adults. However, I think it is important for this to be seen not as 'either/or', but rather as 'both/and'. Just as the couples whom I counsel need assistance to communicate their needs to each other, families also require similar help in order for all members to be heard.

I have attempted in this book to give illustrations both from my own experience as a child and as an adult through my own 'inner child', as well as from my own children and indeed from my work with other people's children. Many of the ideas have been inspired by others' work and have since grown and expanded. However, I alone must take responsibility for emphasizing the importance of play in relation to emergent art. I believe that we must not fall into the trap of thinking that play and art are expendable 'luxury' activities – ample research exists which demonstrates that they are central to human survival and that society is grossly the poorer without them.

I hope that you the reader enjoy playing as much as I do, both in your own world and in that of the children with whom you work. Remember that your own 'inner child' needs nurture and protec-

tion and understanding – only then will you be able to work with
the distressed children of others.

'Mama, mama, golden bees gather about the old man, flying and buz-
zing. Mama, do not weep, I shall make you a present of grace.' (He
throws her a handful of brightness, and the mother's black garments
become covered with golden spots, and luminous little flowers blossom
on the ground).'

(The Child in the Jaws of Night. Fragment of a Planned Mystery
Andrei Bely, 1898 trans. Gerould).

Afterword

At the beginning of Chapter 1 there is sensible concern over rigid categories of development. These are general milestones in development but each one of us is different and so is each child. (Artificial sophistication in the very young now hides much and even alters normal stages of development. On-the-spot contortions replace creative dance with journey and the whole adds up to a certain loss of childhood.) Nevertheless I always used to try and get staff to understand Child Drama in hospitals for adult mental patients, so that if they knew the general development they could assess better where their charges had 'got to' for many of them are childlike. People sometimes get stuck in earlier stages too, largely because of the lack of emotional training in infant schools and early part of juniors. Sometimes one finds students in secondary education who are 'stuck' – to the detriment of themselves and society – and still need to go through earlier stages. The gang starts in the infant school and where it is not known how to promote the Dawn of Seriousness (about 6–7 years) or to make use of it, the wrong tough leader may arise and dominate. This is often the cause of later delinquency.

Chapter 3 has so many good points in it, wonderful advice and examples that I hesitate to comment. But here we have a wide general heading of *Projective* play. One dictionary describes 'projective' as pushing an experience into another realm or experience – physical or mental. I do so want to avoid making confusion in the mind of any reader. But maybe I had better take the bull by the horns and say this has never been quite enough for me. In my own work and philosophy I make a further differentiation. It is that there is a clear and important distinction between what I have termed projected play and personal play. It is true that something projective may, in a general sense be in both, but the balance of personal and projected play in its detailed distinction has great value in each individual and has (as has been said) a link between extravert and introvert. Projected play is where a child's body is somewhat still or almost still and it projects the dream or thought out of its mind into, onto or around objects outside itself. The drama, the dream-life is taking place now in the objects played with. (Sue describes so well how this is beginning to happen at the beginning of the chapter.) But these objects played with may be invested with extreme emotion and stand, as I have so often said and written, as 'monuments of the doing.' Its test is that the man/woman walks away and the memorial of his/her doing (the objects) remains. So, painted pictures, sculpture, pottery, written words or music, cathedrals are all such memorials, all invested with love or importance. Later, some of these turn into symbols such as numbers in the three Rs. It is easier to keep the numbers as representation in a bank than carry and stack individual bags of gold all the time. The absorption the child shows in this type of creation is something to nurture and guard with understanding, as it will help in school work and professional life later.

In personal play the individual gets up and takes full active responsibility for creation with mind and body (no longer can the doll or toy do it for you), and maybe enrolement. Thus acting, running, dancing are all of this realm and it is rather of the extrovert. But having been done, with the full body and enactment, unless filmed or photographed, it is ephemeral, it is gone – disappeared into the mists of time. But the experience is still inside you. No one can take that away. At different periods of life a different proportion of each form of play (or activity) may be needed, until we finally settle down to a general balance of life – each person different. Why the understanding of this is so important in therapy, particularly in child therapy, is that, so often, failure in the projected realm (three Rs) needs tremendous use of personal play, the other extreme, so that real or even imagined victories outweigh the failures. When they have, *that* is the time to return to the projected realm and not before. Mental health is awfully like a bank account. Victories are a plus. Too many failures make an overdraft and interest adds up unless something is done about it.

Under a heading of Directed play there are some carefully selected points about how far the adult should join in. It is easy to miss seeing, or indeed respecting, the value of elementary play and too easy to overdirect. I often use the word 'guide'. One should observe a lot. Experience helps one about when to decide to guide. The adult mind has a necessary place in education and even more in therapy. The examples Sue gives show this. In the home situation children may need time and chance to test out life experiences by themselves quite often. Again, the de-rolement may be necessary for the therapist, if only to clear up for the next child, apart from mental calm and neater psychological finish. But, in the home, let parents consider what has been said about: not to tidy away too quickly. The objects may be returned to; and do consider 'near-finish.' Acting and dancing for pleasure, or as life tests, should be allowed too.

In Chapter 10 there are some wise words on playtherapists being able and having the chance themselves, to play. In my own training I always used to provide much practical work; as well as theory and method by which students could understand purpose, intention and further development. In other words *why* we were doing this and what we were aiming for. So many teachers, or guides, just do exercises that they have seen or read about, with no particular purpose – sometimes with the wrong age, at the wrong time and in the wrong order. The fault is not their's.

I would like to end these comments by further stressing the author's suggestion that potential playtherapists should learn about and face again the child within themselves. This does not mean that they have to be childish and silly. It means they should be imaginative, enthusiastic, humorous, co-operative with other people and taking joy in simple things of the senses, taking joy in good moments of life, recognising that if tomorrow is bad, *this* is good, now! It entails becoming sincere about imaginative situations, developing enjoyable humour and concern for others in a group. Training for it is not easy to find, but that is what I aimed at in directing my summer courses and in the years when running my Child Drama Certificate Course for teachers, nurses, and social workers. We tried to put forward a constructive, purposeful, progressive method and offered a lot of practical work in drama and dance so that people could find themselves again, or discover a new world. Some of it was something like the Stanislavsky 'If' I suppose: if I were *really* that person in that situation (real or Alice-in-Wonderland), what would I think, do, say? So a baby dragon with a bad cold becomes a real problem, not an idea to giggle at, but something that really makes you think. Can it take aspirin? Careful: does it snort fire when it sneezes? What is it like to touch? Can you be really sorry for something that isn't there? You can learn to be and come nearer to childhood again. I can only say that, after the first course, one Head teacher exclaimed, 'I don't know what you will think of the drama, but what *have* you done to the teacher? She is keen now, seems to like children instead of being rude and impatient, stays on late and is constructive and helpful instead of arguing at meetings. She really seems to love her work. It's a miracle.'

Teachers who had been through the Child Drama Certificate Course in the old days and really knew how to guide it with children of different ages and different needs were, to a great extent, in fact, playtherapists though they probably didn't know it.

If you want to be a good playtherapist it helps to be non-judgemental and to be able to slough off sadness. Finally, you should have a non-sentimental objective love of humanity – otherwise, apart from success, it may prove a personal strain on you to do this work.

Sue Jennings should be encouraged in every way, through use of this book and through the courses she and her staff run, to further the cause of playtherapy and to establish it firmly for the greater happiness and health of children everywhere in need.

Peter Slade

Appendix 1

Developmental Checklist

0–3 months
  Skin and touch sensitivity
  Empathy with mother
  Mouth and hand play
  Sound repetition and vocal play
  Surprise at face

3–6 months
  Postural cues
  Movement repetition
  Interest in bodily things
  Interest in faces
  Interest in colours
  Play with food
  Play with toys
  Excitement at familiar things
  Laughs at surprise
  Moves and 'sings' with parent
  Crescendo ('This Little Piggy Went to Market')

6–12 months
  Crawling/walking
  Development of personal circle around body
  Pretends to be mother ('the primal act')
  Anticipates climax
  Makes others audience

Clear purposes, goals
Demands attention
Repetitions
Sound games
Gestural language
Explores objects – realizes their existence
Delight at outcome
'Peek-a-boo'
Jokes

1–2 years
Insatiable curiosity
Mischievousness
'Me' and 'mine'
Exchange with others
Words developing
Dances
Pretence actions
Makes toys pretend
Pretends objects are toys
Relates toys to one another (doll in another toy)
Makes exists and entrances
Carries treasures about
Crayons in fist
Being chased or chasing
Explorations: length/weight/number/size
Makes rules
Makes music in time, rhythm
Makes 'homes' (boxes, cloth)

2–3 years
Movement flexibility: speed, rhythm, up/down, front/back
Strategies (offers, bargains)
Running commentaries
Sentences develop
Complete sequences of action (time)
Personifies parent routines
Time: 'in a minute'/'in a little while'
Group choral games
Crayons in fingers
Joins toys in pretence
Changes roles

Narratives continued
Hide and seek/'house'/tag

3–4 years
'Why?'
Puzzles ('it fits')
Takes turns, sharing
Group games
Good gross motor control
Early grammar
Exaggerated stories
'Follow the leader'
Space differences made
Participates in narratives
Matching games (buttons/boxes)
Makes pretence environments
Runs from 'monsters'
Dressing up
Pretence emotions
Groups of characters played
Acts problems/fairy tales

4–5 years
Fine motor control
Secrets, surprises
Grammar develops
Group pretence play
Early conscience
Friends and enemies
Seeks approval from peers
Highly imaginative roles
Different voices
Symbol distinguished from reality
Gymnastics
Free movement to music
Relay races/creeping
Pretends to tell the time
Games of order ('Ring around a Rosy')
Play rituals (possession, sequences)
Consciousness of roles of others
Puppets
Anticipates future

Invents narrative
Begins to learn to avoid aggression
Relies on own judgment

5–7 years
Learns time beat
Boy/girl/baby play (sex)
Group play
Groups move in large circles
Role flexibility
Social roles begun (teacher/pupil)
Caricature
Games of acceptance ('Farmer in the dell')
Playful conversations
Improvises movements, objects, characters, situations
Analogy/animism
Difficulty in distinguishing fantasy and reality
Makes costumes/clay models
Chasing and running games
Left/right awareness
Realistic themes
Episodic plots (picaresque)
Movement: 'big/small/grow'

7–9 years
Highly creative dance
Can write well
Play with mechanical toys
Collections, crazes, hobbies
Sense of fairness
Card and board games/creates own games
Feeling for ideas of others
Plays exaggerated roles
Distinguishes fantasy and reality
Plots: exaggerated/realistic/surprises/myths/legends/occupations
Establishes improved speech/rich flow/nonsense talk (gibberish)
Puppets and puppet theatres
Groups play in small circles/spirals
Games of dominance ('King of the castle')
Increased grace/speed
Large group improvisation/pairs/solos/leaders emerge
Ball games

Cumulative plots/long endings/abrupt finishes
Group play in horseshoe shape begun
Love of detail

9–13 years

Movement: changes in direction/focus/near and far
Increased clarity in gesture and body shape
Handicrafts
Very co-operative/independent
Winning/losing games
Intellectual games (charades)
Informal concerts
Growth of hypothesis/classification/historical sense
Small group improvisation/good partner work
Fluent speech
Language more important
Creative writing
Small scripts used in some improvisation
Invention of own languages
Use of private codes
Plots of climax and conflict
Themes: animals/adventure/occupations
Emotional characterizations
Social role playing increases/social playmaking
Increasing need to 'show'
Explores real in possible
Space: horseshoe shape developed/end shapes explored

(Reproduced from *Drama in Therapy, Volume 1, Children,* (1981) edited by R. Courtney & G. Schattner, New York, Drama Book Specialists.)

Appendix 2

Playtherapy Methods

EMBODIMENT

Rolling

Free rolling into centre and out again; rolling over other 'bodies'; rolling in 'jelly'; rolling as a log; resisting being rolled; children rolling adult.

Rides and slides

Pulling partner by the ankles; riding on the back; lying on the back and sliding off; pulling self along floor by hands; pushing self along floor by feet; crawling round room over/under others; four people making a bridge/tunnel to crawl over/through.

Shapes

Star-fish – stick to the floor; curling and stretching; star fish and sword dance; making a bridge with hands and feet – going over/under; making a human climbing frame.

Carrying

Piggy or monkey back; rocking on four backs; carrying on four backs.

Sitting

Back-to-back pushing/pulling partner; sitting in threes and travelling across floor; becoming a boat and sailing away in a storm; holding hands with partner and third person tries to get in.

Trust

Rocking a person on four backs; balancing on a back; 'throwing' a person; leaping forwards/backwards in the soft area.

Sensory

Sense box – touch, taste, smell, sight, sound; texture box; feely bag (see Chapter 5); sand and water; water and bubbles; Plasticine and clay; soft toys; slime and jelly.

Container play

Inside large boxes, cushions, Wendy house (see projective container play below).

PROJECTION

Drawing/painting

Finger painting; drawing with crayons/felt pens/pencils; painting patterns, gardens, landscapes, feelings, dreams, stories, people.

Sandplay

Create a story, a 'World', a picture, a building, a house, a landscape; free texture/sense play.

Sculpting

Create with small toys (people/animals/transport/'treasures') a picture or story or family.
Larger toys/puppets/cushions – an environment, a house/castle, a family.
Nesting dolls: family scenes and dynamics.

'Natural objects' create scenes and landscapes.
Create a picture from textures.

Container play

Journey box: create a 'contained' landscape and tell the journey (Chapter 5); treasure box; boxes inside boxes; nesting dolls.

ROLE

Mimicry: sounds, gestures, reaction.
Pretend: to be mother, dog, monster.
Personify: mother, family members, TV characters (variation not just replication), role taking.
Projective roles: through puppets, objects, animals.
Enactment: enact roles and scenes; dramatize the story; role reversal; therapist 'in role'; creating a new ending for story.
Dramatic play: separation of enactment from other play activities; dressing up family and social scenes.
Drama: incorporates all of the above ideas tested, aesthetic sense and artistry, creativity, originality, flexibility and problem solving.
Drama starters: large collection of postcards – scenes, people, landscapes.

STORIES

The Log Story, The Magic Forest, The Boat Story (Chapter 2)
Oseo (Chapter 5)

The above playtherapy techniques are all described in this book. If they are unfamiliar, it is wise to test them on your friends or your own children until you feel confident.

Further methods are described in:

Barker, C. (1977) *Theatre Games*. London: Eyre Methuen.
Jennings, S. (1986) *Creative Drama in Groupwork*. Bicester: Winslow Press.
Sherborne, V. (1990) *Developmental Movement for Children*. Cambridge: Cambridge University Press.

Note: once you feel confident in the playtherapy milieu, the children themselves assist you to develop your repertoire of methods.

A Training Programme for Playtherapists

It is only recently that playtherapy both in the UK and overseas is being recognized in its own right as a professional practice rather than being a part of other disciplines and practices. Most professionals who work with children have some play method included in their training and child psychoanalysts have extended experience in psychoanalytically orientated play.

The Institute of Dramatherapy has offered training in the Playtherapy Method since 1986 and the following is the syllabus for both the certificate and diploma courses. Those who wish to have a recognized qualification follow the Diploma in Dramatherapy with a specialism in work with children, though it is expected that a parallel qualification in playtherapy will shortly be available.

PLAYTHERAPY CERTIFICATE OR FOUNDATION COURSE

Syllabus

An introduction to dramatic play and play with rules together with accompanying theory from psychology and drama.
An introduction to developmental psychology and child and adolescent psychiatry.
An introduction to the healing metaphor; the use of fairy tales in diagnosis and practice, 6PSM.
Students undertake observations of child development as well as childrens' play. Assessed through written work.

PLAYTHERAPY DIPLOMA COURSE

Syllabus

Playtherapy method and application, EPR in assessment and practice. Planning a programme stage 1.
Clinical theory: object relations theory, transitional phenomena, attachment theory.
Healing metaphor: fairy tale – short term intervention.
Playtherapy and sandplay: Jung and Lowenfeld.
Playtherapy application: child abuse, post-traumatic stress disorder, separation and loss.
Playtherapy practice and supervision – trainees carry out practice under regular supervision.
Personal therapy – all trainees undertake personal therapy in which to explore their 'inner child'.

The course is assessed through diagnostic and practice reports, as well as a dissertation which brings together theory and practice.

Course aims

- to provide an introduction to the theory and practice of the Playtherapy Method.
- to provide a multi-model approach to intervention.
- to develop the concept of the healing metaphor.
- to address the issues of child trauma and appropriate intervention.
- to ensure appropriate supervision of practice and adequate personal therapy for the practitioner.
- to address the issues of codes of practice and ethics.

More information on training can be obtained from:

(1) Playtherapy Training, Faculty of Arts and Humanities, Roehampton Institute, Digby Stuart College, Roehampton Lane, London SW15 5PH. Tel. 081 392 3064.
(2) Association of Play Therapists, Lynn Bennett, Bucklands Cottage, Wallingford Road, Cholsey, Oxon, OX10 9HB.
(3) Dramatherapy Consultants, PO Box 32, Stratford-upon-Avon CV37 6GU. Tel. 0789 268558.

Bibliography and Further Reading

BIBLIOGRAPHY

Axline, V. (1947); *Play Therapy* revised (1969) New York: Ballantine Books.
Axline, V. (1964) *Dibs in Search of Self*. London: Penguin.
Behar, D. & Rapaport, J.L. (1983) 'Play observation and psychiatric diagnosis' In C.E. Schaefer and K. O'Connor (Eds) *Handbook of Playtherapy*. New York: John Wiley.
Berry, C. (1975) *Your Voice and How to Use it Successfully*. London: Harrap.
Block, D. (1978) *So the Witch Won't Eat Me*. New York: Grove Press.
Brook, P. (1968) *The Empty Space*. Harmondsworth: Penguin.
Brook, P. (1988) *The Shifting Point*. London: Methuen.
Brudenell, P. (1986) *The Other Side of Profound Handicap*. London: Macmillan.
Bruner, J.S., Jolly, A. & Sylva, K. (1976) (Eds) *Play: Its Role in Development*. Harmondsworth: Penguin.
Cattanach, A. (1992) *Playtherapy with Abused Children*. London: Jessica Kingsley.
Chukovsky, K. (1963) 'The sense of nonsense verse' In Bruner op. cit.
Courtney, R. (1982) Re-play. Toronto: OISE Press.
Courtney, R. & Schattner, G. (1981) *Drama in Therapy. Volume 1. Children*. New York: Drama Book Specialists.
Cox, M. & Theilgaard, A. (1987) (Eds) *Mutative Metaphors in Psychotherapy*. London: Tavistock Publications.
Cox, M. (1989) *Structuring the Therapeutic Process: Compromise with Chaos*. London: Jessica Kingsley.
Davis, J. (1991) Introduction to *Play in Childhood* by M. Lowenfeld. London: MacKeith Press.
Dodd, N. & Hickson, W. (1971) (Eds) *Drama and Theatre in Education*. London: Heinemann Educational.
Edgar, D. (1978) Mary Barnes: A Play. London: Methuen.
Erikson, E. (1965) Childhood in Society. Harmondsworth: Penguin.

Euripides, trans. Vellacott, P. (1963) *Medea/Hecate/Electra/Heracles*. Harmondsworth: Penguin Books.

Feilden, T. (1990) 'Art therapy as part of the world of dyslexic children' In M. Liebmann (Ed) *Art Therapy in Practice*. London: Jessica Kingsley.

Fordham, M. (1986) *Jungian Psychotherapy*. London: Maresfield.

Franz, M., von (1974) *Shadow and Evil in Fairytales*. Dallas: Spring.

Franz, M., von (1987) *The Interpretation of Fairytales*. Dallas: Spring.

Garvey, C. (1977) *Play*. Glasgow: Fontana.

Garvey, C. (1984) *Children's Talk*. Oxford: Fontana.

Gersie, A. (1991) *Story Making in Bereavement*. London: Jessica Kingsley.

Gleitman, H. (1986) *Psychology*. New York: Norton.

Heathcote, D. (1981) 'Drama and the mentally handicapped' In G. Lord (Ed) *The Arts and Disabilities*. London: Macmillan.

Henry, J. & Henry, Z. (1974) *Doll Play of Pilaga Indian Children*. New York: Vintage Books.

Hillman, J. (1983) *Healing Fiction*. New York: Station Hill Press.

Irwin, E. (1983) 'The diagnostic and therapeutic use of pretend play' In C.E. Schaefer and K. O'Connor (Ed) *Handbook of Playtherapy*. New York: John Wiley.

Jacobson, E. (1964) *The Self and the Object World*. New York: International Universities Press.

Jacques, P. (1987) *Children's Problems*. London: Unwin.

Jansson, T. (1962) *Tales From Moominvalley*. London: Puffin.

Jennings, S. (1973) *Remedial Drama*. London: A & C Black.

Jennings, S. (1986) *Creative Drama in Groupwork*. Bicester: Winslow Press.

Jennings, S. (1987) (Ed) *Dramatherapy Theory and Practice*. London: Routledge.

Jennings, S. (1989) The Trying Time: Dramatherapy with Adolescents. In Jones (Ed) *Special Educational Needs Review*. London and New York: Falmer Press.

Jennings, S. (1990) *Dramatherapy with Families, Groups and Individuals*. London: Jessica Kingsley.

Jennings, S. (1992) *Dramatherapy Theory and Practice, Vol. 2*. London: Routledge.

Jennings, S. (in preparation) *Theatre, Ritual and Transformation*. London: Routledge.

Jung, C.G. (1967) *Memories, Dreams, Reflections*. London: Routledge.

Kalff, D. (1980) *Sandplay*. Santa Monica: Sigo Press.

Kernberg, O. (1984) *Object-Relations Theory and Clinical Psychoanalysis*. New York: Jason Aronson.

Kitzinger, S. (1978) *Women as Mothers*. Glasgow: Fontana/Collins.

Lahad, M. (1992) 'Story making and assessment methods for coping with stress: six-part story making and BASIC Ph' In S. Jennings (Ed) *Dramatherapy Theory and Practice, Vol. 2*. London: Routledge.

Landy, R. (1986) *Drama Therapy*. Illinois: Charles C. Thomas Publications.

Liebmann, M. (Ed) (1990) *Art Therapy in Practice*. London: Jessica Kingsley.

Lord, G. (Ed) (1981) *The Arts and Disabilities*. London: Macmillan.

Lord, G. (Ed) (1985) *The Arts and Disabilities: the Attenborough Report*. London: Bedford Square Press.

Lowenfeld, M. (1935) *Play in Childhood*. London: MacKeith Press.

Matterson, E.M. (1975) *Play with a Purpose for Under Sevens*. Harmondsworth: Penguin.

McCaslin, N. (1981) *Children and Drama*. New York and London: Longman.

McClintock, A. (1984) *Drama for Mentally Handicapped Children*. London: Souvenir Press.

Miller, A. (1981) *The Drama of Being a Child*. London: Virago Press.

Miller, A. (1990) *The Untouched Key*. London: Virago Press.

Milne, A.A. (1924) *When We Were Very Young*. London: Methuen.

Moray Williams, U. (1938) *The Adventures of the Little Wooden Horse*. London: Harrap.

Napier, A.D. (1986) *Masks, Transformation and Paradox*. London: University of California Press.

Neumann, E. (1973) *The Child*. London: Hodder & Stoughton.

Oaklander, V. (1978) *Windows to our Children*. Moab, Utah: Real People Press.

Opie, I. & P. (1959) *The Lore and Language of Schoolchildren*. Oxford: Oxford University Press.

Papadatou, D. & Papadatos, C. (1991) (Eds) *Children and Death*. London: Hemisphere Publishing.

Piaget, J. (1962) Play, *Dreams and Imitation in Childhood*. London: Routledge.

Reed J. Pruyn (1975) *Sand Magic*. Albuquerque: JPR Publications.

Robinson, G. & Hill, D. (1973) *Coyote the Trickster*. London: Pan Books.

Rycroft, C. (1985) *Psychoanalysis and Beyond*. London: Chatto & Windus.

Saint-Exupery, A., de (1982) *The Little Prince*. London: Pan Books.

Schaefer, C. & O'Connor, K. (1983) (Eds) *Handbook of Play Therapy*. New York: John Wiley.

Shakespeare, W. (1980) *Hamlet*. London: Penguin Books.

Sherborne, V. (1975) Chapter in *Creative Therapy*. (Ed. S. Jennings) DTC.

Sherborne, V. (1990) *Developmental Movement for Children*. Cambridge: Cambridge University Press.

Sidoli, M. & Davies, M. (1988) (Eds) *Jungian Child Psychotherapy*. London: Karnac Books.

Slade, P. (1954) *Child Drama*. London: University of London Press.

Slade, P. (1958) *An Introduction to Child Drama*. London: Hodder & Stoughton.

Smilansky, S. (1968) *The Effects of Sociodramatic Play on Disadvantaged Pre-School Children*. New York: John Wiley.

Steinberg, D. (1987) *Basic Adolescent Psychiatry*. Oxford: Blackwell Scientific.

Steinberg, D. (1989) *Interprofessional Consultation*. Oxford: Blackwell Scientific.

Steinberg, D. (1981) *Using Child Psychiatry*. Sevenoaks: Hodder & Stoughton.

Tomlinson, R. (1982) *Disability Theatre and Education*. London: Souvenir Press.

Wagner, B.J. (1979) *Dorothy Heathcote Drama as a Learning Medium*. London: Hutchinson Educational.

Way, B. (1967) *Development Through Drama*. London: Longman.

Weinrib, E. (1983) *Images of the Self*. Boston: Sigo Press.

Weir (1962) *Playing with Language*. In Bruner op. cit.

Winnicott, D.W. (1964) *The Child, the Family and the Outside World*. Harmondsworth: Penguin.

Winnicott, D.W. (1971) *Playing and Reality*. Harmondsworth: Penguin.

Winnicott, D.W. (1975) *Through Pediatrics to Psychoanalysis*. London: Hogarth Press.

FURTHER READING

I would draw the readers attention to Cattanach (1992) *Playtherapy with Abused Children*, which I have referred to in several chapters in this book, in relation to playtherapy practice. It has also has an excellent bibliography and list of books for children themselves as well as a useful overview of current legislation. Also West (1992) *Child-Centred Play Therapy* has an extensive bibliography as well as useful questions for playtherapists to ask themselves about their practice.

The following selective titles I have found useful in my own work:

Ariel, S. (1992) *Strategic Family Play Therapy*. Chichester: John Wiley.

Brun, B., Pedersen, E.W. and Runberg, M. (1992) *Symbols of the Soul: Therapy and Guidance through Fairy Tales*. London: Jessica Kingsley

Davis, M. and Wallbridge, D. (1981) *Boundary and Space: An Introduction to the Work of D W Winnicott*. London: H. Karnac.

Hansen, T. (1991) *Seven for a Secret: Healing the Wounds of Sexual Abuse in Childhood*. London: Triangle/SPCK.

Jennings, S. (1988) 'The loneliness of the long distance therapist'. *British Journal of Psychotherapy* Vol. 4 No. 3.

Jennings, S. (1993) *Introduction to Dramatherapy*. London: Jessica Kingsley.

Lahad, M. (1988) *Community Stress Prevention*. Kiriat Shmona, Israel: Community Stress Prevention Centre.

Lahad, M. and Gersie, A. (in preparation) *The Healing Metaphor*. London: Jessica Kingsley.

Lowenfeld, M. (1979) *The World Technique*. London: Allen and Unwin.

Miller, A. (1987) *For Your Own Good: The Roots of Violence in Child-rearing*. London: Virago.

Minde, A. and Jennings, S. (1993) *Art Therapy and Dramatherapy: Masks of the Soul*. London: Jessica Kingsley.

Minuchin, S. (1984) *Family Kaleidoscope*. Cambridge, Mass. and London, UK: Harvard University Press.

Parks, P. (1990) *Rescuing the Inner Child*. London: Souvenir Press.

Post, L. van der (1961) *The Heart of the Hunter*. London: Penguin.

Ryce-Menuhin, J. (1992) *Jungian Sandplay: The Wonderful Therapy*. London: Routledge.

West, J. (1992) *Child-Centred Play Therapy*. London: Edward Arnold.

Index

210